12 Steps To Overcoming Tragic Life Events

The Way, The Truth, and The Life
(John 14:6)

Dr. Julia Floyd Jones

WESTBOW
P R E S S®
A DIVISION OF THOMAS NELSON
& ZONDERVAN

Scripture taken from the King James Version of the Bible.

Scripture taken from the New King James Version®. Copyright © 1982 by Thomas Nelson. Used by permission. All rights reserved.

WestBow Press books may be ordered through booksellers or by contacting:

WestBow Press
A Division of Thomas Nelson & Zondervan
1663 Liberty Drive
Bloomington, IN 47403
www.westbowpress.com
1-(866) 928-1240

ISBN: 978-1-4497-6509-5 (sc)
ISBN: 978-1-4497-6510-1 (e)

Library of Congress Control Number: 2012916209

Print information available on the last page.

WestBow Press rev. date: 04/04/2019

Contents

Preface

This is not another "anonymous" twelve step program. This book is biblically based and is synonymous with the unadulterated Word of the living God. Not a book about a self-defined higher power but about the power of the Most High God.

Twelve Steps To Overcoming Tragic Life Events is an instruction manual to get you out of bondage. Follow God's directives as written in this book, your Bible and through the revelation knowledge that you receive as a result of your study in the Word.

This book will not only inspire you but it will change you as you allow the Creator to forever change you, heal you, and mold you through His Word. To God be the glory.

Julia Floyd Jones, Ph.D.

Foreword

Before you begin you will need a Holy Bible and a journal to complete the assignments for each chapter. Scriptures quoted in this text are from the King James version unless otherwise stated. Although space is allocated in the book for your responses it is not necessary to limit your responses to the space provided. You may hand write your answers in a journal or keep an electronic journal if that is your preference. Record the time and date of each entry so that in later times you will come to see a pattern of when you are most receptive to the voice of God. You will have a time log of when your prayers were both spoken and answered. It is important to be thorough and honest so that you will obtain the maximum benefit from this book.

After you complete Step Four start writing your life story. Start from the beginning, this is your autobiography.

As you recall your life events, you may get anxious or experience other uncomfortable feelings. If this occurs take time to pause, and write down how you feel. Read one of the prayers in Appendix A if you are not able to calm down on your own or listen to music. Appendix B contains healing scriptures, and use Appendix C to record answered prayers.

It may take you several weeks or several months to complete this book. This book was written to guide you down your road to recovery. Your recovery may be slow and arduous or quick and painless or somewhere in between. It is important to stay on the road to recovery no matter what the circumstances. Use the rest stops along the way (suggested prayers in Appendix A) and re-fuel as needed (Bible references in each chapter). The end of the road will bring you to your destination of healing and freedom from the past.

Introduction

Tragedy is defined as a disastrous event, calamity, or misfortune (Webster, 1998). During one's lifetime it is highly probable that tragedy will strike, if not to us personally, but to family, friends, or co-workers. We live in a world where natural and man-made disasters occur on a regular basis. You may have experienced a terrible divorce, lost a loved one, have a physical defect, suffer from a mental illness or an addiction, been demoted or fired from a job. If you have unresolved issues that are causing you distress then this book is for you. How you experience the tragedy may be different from others who have had similar experiences. Your perceptions, and feelings surrounding the event may not be expressed where others may understand or empathize. That does not matter. What matters is how you feel and your willingness to get well.

Tragic events may cause trauma (injury) to the body and mind. However, not everyone that experiences a tragedy will sustain long-term trauma. Mental trauma can be experienced immediately after the event or the symptoms may appear months or even years later. For example panic disorder or posttraumatic stress disorder are often experienced months or years after the initial tragedy (Van der Kolk, McFarlane, & Weisaaeth, 1996).

There is also the misperception that unspoken events are forgotten events, or that children under the age of five will not remember traumatic events. This is simply not true. The human brain is capable of recording and storing everything that has happened to you in your lifetime. Encoding of memory involves the sensory mechanisms of taste, smell, sight, hearing, and touch. Many of us are not able to recall certain memories at will. Often past memories are triggered by recent events that are similar in nature to the past event through the sensory mechanisms that remind us of the past events (Mastin, 2010)

Memories often disguise themselves and come in the form of nightmares, flashbacks, or intrusive thoughts (Van der Kolk, McFarlane, & Weisaaeth, 1996). If you are experiencing any of these symptoms it is highly recommended that you consult with a Christian mental health professional so that you are provided with adequate support and counseling as you work through this book.

In the space provided or in your journal write down your tragic life events and/or the issues that are causing distress in your life right now. Be specific and limit your response to a paragraph or less.

_____

_____

_____

After you have written your response, record the time and date so that you will have a record of your progress. Do this before and after each step.

Now you are ready to begin your step work. Take your time. Read thoughtfully and deliberately. Although I have listed the Bible verses in the text, it is suggested that you use your own Bible to look up the verses. Read and meditate on the scripture references. Let God lead you. This is one way in which the most High God will speak to you, through His Word.

STEP ONE

SAY "THE NAME"

J esus is the name. Say the name of the one who created you. He is the Alpha and the Omega, the first and the last. The Lord spoke you into being, He created you before the foundation of the world. He planned you, He purposed you, He ordained you. It does not matter what has happened to you in the past. The one true living God can fix it all. He can mend your broken heart, heal your mind and your body. Put faith into action and say "the name" with boldness, **JESUS!**

> *In whom we have boldness and access with confidence by the faith of him (Ephesians 3:12).*

It is important to understand that God is a triune God. God the Father, God the Son, and God the Holy Spirit. *For there are three that bear record in heaven, the Father, the Word, and the Holy Ghost, and these three are one (I John 5:7)* **God the Creator.** *In the beginning God created the heaven and the earth (Genesis 1:1). In the beginning was the Word, and the Word was with God, and the Word was God. The same was in the beginning with God. All things were made by him, and without him was not anything made that was made. In him was life and the life was the light of men. And the light shineth in darkness and the darkness comprehended it not (John 1:1-5). For the Lord your God is God of gods, and Lord of lords, a great God, a mighty God (Deuteronomy 10:17).* God is the ultimate higher power, always present, all knowing, and all powerful.

Jesus the Son of God, who is all God and all man. Let the following verses speak to your heart. *For God so loved the world, that he gave his only begotten Son, that whosoever believeth in him should not perish but have everlasting life (John 3:16). For through him we both have access by one Spirit unto the Father (Ephesians 2:18). Who is gone into heaven and is on the right hand of God, angels and authorities and powers being made subject unto him (I Peter 3:22).* Jesus is ready to have a relationship with you, receive Him now.

When the world's way no longer works for you and you are at your wit's end, do not give up. **The Holy Spirit** will guide you. *But the Comforter, which is the Holy Ghost, whom the Father will send in my name, he shall teach you all things, and bring all things to your remembrance, whatsoever I have said unto you* (John 14:26). *Ye shall be baptized with the Holy Ghost (Acts 1:5b) but the anointing which ye have received of him abideth in you, and ye need not that any man teach you but as the same anointing teacheth you of all things, and is truth (I John 2:27), because the spirit is truth (I John 5:6b).*

When you don't know what to say, when you become so overwhelmed with the situation at hand let the Holy Spirit intercede for you and empower you. *Ye shall receive power, after that the Holy Ghost is come upon you (Acts 1:8a). And they were all filled with the Holy Ghost, and began to speak with other tongues, as the Spirit gave them utterance (Acts 2:4).* The Holy Spirit is the comforter, the counselor, and the teacher. He is everything you need him to be, and everywhere you need Him to be, you are never truly alone or left to your own devices.

Some of you may have been taught differently about who God is. Don't let your theology get in the way of your healing. Keep reading. The Lord is with you. He wants to make you whole. Receive that by faith.

So then faith cometh by hearing, and hearing by the word of God (Romans 10:17).

The Names of God

God has many names, the great I AM, Yahweh, and many more. Peruse the following list of names and their meanings and then read the scripture that corresponds with the names of God. As you read the verses you will develop a more intimate communication with God. Describe the situation and its relevance to the name of God.

Example: **Jehovah-Jireh**—*The Lord will provide.* When I lost my job, I prayed daily that God would provide for my family.

We always had food and shelter. Even when the cupboards were bare, friends and family would invite us over for dinner. We never went one day without a meal. For that Lord, I thank you.

Names of God	Meaning and Verses
Adonai	**The Lord, My Great Lord (Psalm 8)** O Lord our Lord how excellent is they name in all the earth who hast set thy glory above the heavens.
El	**The Strong One (Exodus 15:2)** The Lord is my strength and song and he is become my salvation, he is my God and I will prepare him a habitation, my father's God, and I will exalt him.
El Elohe Yisrael	**God, The God of Israel (Genesis 33:20)** And he erected there an altar and called it El Elohe Israel.
Elohim	**The All-Powerful One, Creator (Daniel 4:34)** And at the end of the days I Nebuchadnezzer lifted up mine eyes unto heaven and mine understanding returned unto me and I blessed the most High and I praised and honored him that liveth for ever, whose dominion and his kingdom is from generation to generation.
El Olam	**The Eternal God, The Everlasting God (Isaiah40:28)** Hast thou not known, hast thou not heard that the everlasting God, the Lord the Creator of the ends of the earth fainteth not, neither is weary? There is no searching of his understanding.

El Roi	**The God Who Sees Me (Genesis 16:13)** And she called the name of the Lord that spake unto her, Thou God seest me for she said, have I also here looked after him that seeth me?
El Shaddai	**The All Sufficient One, God of the Mountains (Genesis 17:1)** And when Abram was ninety years old and nine the Lord appeared to Abram and said unto him, I am the Almighty God, walk before me and be thou perfect.
Immanuel	**God With Us (Isaiah 7:14)** Therefore the Lord himself shall give you a sign, Behold a virgin shall conceive and bear a son and shall call his name Immanuel.
Jehovah	**I Am, The One Who Is, The Self-Existent One (Exodus 3:14)** And God said unto Moses, I am that I am, and he said thus shalt thou say unto the children of Israel, I am hath sent me unto you.
Jehovah-Jireh	**The Lord Will Provide (Genesis 22:13, 14)** Abraham lifted up his eyes and looked and behold behind him a ram caught in a thicket by his horns and Abraham went and took the ram and offered him up for a burnt offering in the stead of his son. And Abraham called the name of the place Jehovah-Jireh as it is said to this day. In the mount of the Lord it shall be seen.

Jehovah-Mekaddishkem	**The Lord Who Sanctifies (Exodus 31:13)** Speak thou also unto the children of Israel saying, verily my Sabbaths ye shall keep for it is a sign between me and you throughout your generations that ye may know that I am the Lord that doth sanctify you.
Jehovan-Nissi	**The Lord is My Banner (Exodus 17:15, 16)** Moses built an altar and called the name of it Jehovah-Nissi. For he said, because the Lord hath sworn that the Lord will have war with Amalek from generation to generation.
Jehovah-Rapha	**The Lord Who Heals (Psalm 103:3)** Who forgiveth all thine iniquities, who healeth all thy diseases.
Jehovah-Rohi	**The Lord is My Shepherd (Psalm 23:1)** The Lord is my shepherd I shall not want.
Jehovah-Sabaoth	**The Lord of Hosts, The Lord of Armies (I Samuel 1:3)** And this man went up out of his city yearly to worship and to sacrifice unto the Lord of hosts in Shiloh.
Jehovah-Shalom	**The Lord is Peace (Numbers 6:26-27)** The Lord lift up his countenance upon thee and give thee peace. And they shall put my name upon the children of Israel and I will bless them.
Jehovah-Shammah	**The Lord is There, The Lord My Companion (Ezekiel 48:35)** It was round about eighteen thousand measures and the name of the city from that day shall be the Lord is there.

Jehovah-Tsidkenu	**The Lord Our Righteousness (Jeremiah 23:6)** In his days Judah shall be saved and Israel shall dwell safely and this is his name whereby he shall be called The Lord Our Righteousness.
Yah or Jah	**I Am, The One Who is The Self-Existent One (Isaiah 26:4)** Trust ye the Lord forever, for in the Lord Jehovah is everlasting strength.
YHWH (pronounced Yah-way)	**I Am, The One Who is The Self-Existent One (Malachi 3:6)** For I am the Lord I change not.

(Rose Publishing, 2003, 2005)

These are the names of God as revealed in the Old Testament. We will study the names of God as written in the New Testament in Step Eleven.

Names and Identity

As shown in this section God identified Himself in several ways depending on the needs of the people. Your identity and name are important as well. Go to a website of your choice and find out the meaning of your first and last name and determine if you have the characteristics of your names. For example; the name Dolores means sorrow and pain, and the name Lloyd is a variation of the name lion. Lions are described as being bold and courageous leaders.

Your identity comprises the sum of who you are and how you perceive and accept different aspects of yourself. They include but are not limited to your; religion, profession, ethnicity, education, family, and reputation. As you grow older and wiser and deeply rooted in the Lord your identity will change.

In order for Abram and Sarai to fulfill their destiny and all the Lord had for them He had to change their names. When Abram was ninety-nine years old God made a covenant with him and promised that he would be the father of many nations. God changed his name from Abram, exalted father, to Abraham, father of many nations. As a sign of the covenant God commanded that Abram and all of his seed throughout the generations be circumcised. At the age of ninety Sarai, which means princess, was to be re-named Sarah or mother of nations. Please read more about this in Genesis chapters 16-20 which illustrates how identity and names coincide.

After Jacob wrestled with an angel, God changed his name to Israel. Overnight his name and identity changed from that of deceiver to one of prince (Genesis 32:38, 35:10). The book of Genesis gives many examples of how every day people struggled with their identity, opposing forces, and who God called them to be.

From the scriptures it is evident that names have the power to shape your identity as well as your destiny. The Lord may be urging you to change your given name, surname, or your business name. He may be prompting you to change jobs which may result in a different job title, or working or living in a different city, etc. Pay attention and listen to what the Lord wants to change to help propel you into your destiny.

God Box

Now that you have a better understanding of who God is it is time to create a God Box. Use a container of your choosing and decorate it. I use this before meetings or with groups and I ask all participants to write down the people they want to pray for or any personal issues they are struggling with. This is essential in your daily walk with the Lord. Write down your worries and concerns and contain or manage them by lifting them up to the Lord. This is a great way to build trust in the Lord and to teach yourself and others to rest in the peace of God as you give Him your cares for the day. This works well for people of all ages at home or in Sunday school classes.

Dear God Letters

Dear God letters are a great addition to your journal. When you feel like pouring your heart out to God then this is a perfect time to write Him a letter. You may not be able to be completely honest with your friends but you can be completely honest with the Lord. He will never betray your trust or gossip about you when you have chosen to write about what He already knows.

The next step in God Letters is to allow the Lord to write back to you. There are many voices out there so make sure that you read your Bible several times per week to ensure that you are connecting with the one true Living God. Every one hears God in a different way. Some people have heard an audible still small voice, some will have thoughts or a sense of knowing that comes from the Lord. Others connect with the Lord with pen and paper and will write down what the Lord is communicating to them. This is another way to keep a record of what the Lord is telling you and how He is maturing your spiritual growth. You start the letter with Dear (your name), and proceed to write what the Lord is communicating to you. Don't worry about punctuation or grammatical errors. From experience I can tell you when the Spirit starts flowing it will be hard to keep up if you try to make corrections as you go along or question what you are writing. Once you finish you can add commas, periods, or correct spelling if it will help but don't feel obligated to do so. This letter is not for publication it is for purification.

Has your concept of God changed in any way?

_____

_____

What names of God are you going to use to describe your relationship with the Most High God?

_____

_____

STEP TWO

CONFESS THAT JESUS IS THE SON OF GOD

This step shows you how to use the name of Jesus. The name of Jesus will have more power if you have been born again. If there is some doubt or confusion about whether or not that you are, say the following prayer out loud:

Prayer For Salvation

I believe in my heart and confess with my mouth that Jesus is the son of God. I believe that He died on the cross for me and rose the third day. Your Word says that whosoever shall call upon the name of the Lord shall be saved (Acts 2:21). Heavenly Father I repent for all the sins I committed knowingly and unknowingly and I forgive everyone who hurt me. I ask Jesus to come into my heart, to cleanse me of all impurities, and to make me brand new. In Jesus' name I pray. Amen.

Take a moment to meditate on the Word by sitting with your eyes closed. Ask Jesus to speak to you, let Him fill your heart with joy. Let Him drop into your soul that inner peace that can only come from God. God chooses to communicate in several different ways. If He has shown you something, spoken to you, or dropped something into your spirit, take this time to write it down below or in your journal.

By praying that prayer you are now a joint heir with the Lord Jesus Christ. You have what He has. All power in heaven in earth has been given to you. You have the mind of Christ. You are free from the law of sin and death. You have been delivered from the spirit of darkness and you have eternal life in Christ Jesus. Hallelujah to the Son of God!

Every tongue should confess that Jesus Christ is Lord, to the glory of God the Father (Philippians 2:11).

The Authority Of The Name

Authority is defined as the power or right to give orders, make decisions, and enforce obedience and to control (Webster, 1998).

Think about the people and institutions that have authority over you or the ways you succumb to authority in certain situations. Law enforcement has the authority to enforce the laws in their designated area by writing tickets, making arrests, or using deadly force, etc.

Your teachers, medical staff, or supervisors have been given authority according to the policy and procedures that have been established by the institutions in which they are employed. When they were hired they agreed to abide by the rules or to face disciplinarian action or termination for infractions.

When you became a born-again believer in Jesus Christ you were given the right to use the authority of the name of Jesus, because there is power in his name.

Wherefore God also hath highly exalted him, and given him a name which is above every name. That at the name of Jesus every knee should bow, of things in heaven, and things in earth, and things under the earth (Philippians 2:9-10).

We have the authority to make spiritual arrest, to claim our kingdom inheritance and to take it by force, to bind the enemy, and to cast him out. We have the power and authority to anoint others with oil, lay hands on the sick, speak in diverse tongues, and pray according to our policy and procedures manual which is the Holy Bible.

Jesus rules and reigns at the right hand of the Father and we are governed by the Kingdom of Heaven as written in scripture. It is our choice whether or not we will obey the mandates of heaven. By using His name you will be able to break free of the strongholds that are keeping you bound. If you are suffering from a mental or physical disease or some type of addiction, your freedom from your affliction is at hand. Some of you may be suffering in other ways. Perhaps you are not able to sleep at night, you have problems at work or in your personal life, or maybe you have been abused in some way. Whatever your discomfort, the Lord can heal and make you whole. Let Him lead you into inner healing from those deep, dark wounds.

Who You Are In Christ

You are important to God. He loves you and wants the best for you. The Lord wants you to understand who He is and how you fit into the Kingdom of God. As a Christian it is important that you represent the Kingdom with honesty and integrity. Christianity is more than a religion it is a lifestyle. Are your co-workers, teammates, neighbors, and classmates able to distinguish you from non-Christians or back-slidden Christians?

The book of Ephesians will help you understand who you are in Christ but I will only include a few scriptures to get you started. This is a great book to study on your own as it will build your character and improve all of your relationships. Feel free to use a version of the Bible that you can understand so that the instructions will make more sense to you. After you read each section write down what the Lord is saying to you through his Word.

...walk not as other Gentiles walk in the vanity of their mind. Having the understanding darkened, being alienated from the life of God through the ignorance that is in them because of the blindness of their heart. Who have given themselves over unto

lasciviousness to work all uncleanness with greediness. But ye have not so learned Christ, if so be that ye have heard him and have been taught by him as the truth is in Jesus. That ye put off concerning former conversations, the old man, which is corrupt according to the deceitful lusts. And be renewed in the spirit of your mind, and that ye put on the new man which after God is created in righteousness and true holiness. (Ephesians 4:17-24).

Wherefore putting away lying, speak every man truth with his neighbors for we are members one of another. Be ye angry and sin not, let not the sun go down upon your wrath, neither give place to the devil. Let him that stole steal no more but rather let him labor working with his hands the thing which is good that he may have to give to him that needeth. Let no corrupt communication proceed out of your mouth but that which is good to the use of edifying that it may minister grace unto the hearers. And grieve not the holy Spirit of God whereby ye are sealed unto the day of redemption. Let all bitterness and wrath and anger and clamor and evil speaking be put away from you with all malice. And be ye kind one to another, tenderhearted, forgiving one another, even as God for Christ's sake hath forgiven you (Ephesians 4:25-32).

. . . the Father of our Lord Jesus Christ of whom the whole family in heaven and earth is named. That he would grant you according to the riches of his glory to be strengthened with might by his Spirit in the inner man. That Christ may dwell

in your hearts by faith that ye being rooted and grounded in love may be able to comprehend with all saints what is the breadth, and length, and depth and height, and to know the love of Christ which passeth knowledge that ye might be filled with all the fullness of God (Ephesians 3:14b, 15-19).

The God of our Lord Jesus Christ, the Father of glory may give unto you the spirit of wisdom and revelation in the knowledge of him. The eyes of your understanding being enlightened, that ye may know what is the hope of his calling and what the riches of the glory of his inheritance in the saints. And what is the exceeding greatness of his mighty power (Ephesians 1:17-19).

And hath raised us up together and made us sit together in heavenly places in Christ Jesus. That in ages to come he might shew the exceeding riches of his grace in his kindness toward us through Christ Jesus (Ephesians 2:6-7).

> ### *Be Still And Know That I Am God*
> (Psalm 46:10a)

STEP THREE

REPENT FOR YOUR TRANSGRESSIONS

When the Bible talks about transgressions it is talking about sin or rebellion. If you are old enough to read this book and work the steps then at some point in your life you have committed sin and rebelled against God or human authority.

In this section list the things you have done that were sinful or rebellious in nature. Include instances that you consider trivial or minuscule occurrences. For example, if you used to steal or failed to tell your neighbor the entire truth when you hit their car while you were backing out of the driveway, include instances like that. Also include negative attitudes that are effecting your social or occupational functioning.

It may be easier for you to start with the present and work backwards. Take your time and list transgressions from your entire life. This exercise depends on the memories you are able to recall. What you remember and what the Holy Ghost brings to your remembrance will suffice. Allow the unconscious to become conscious. Give yourself permission to remember. As you begin to write, one memory will lead to another. Give yourself at least one week to complete this exercise.

List transgressions below or in your journal:

_____

_____

_____

Look for patterns to the type of sin/rebellion, frequency of sin/rebellion, when you started and stopped the behavior or whether or not it is ongoing.

_____

_____

_____

In order to become more like Christ it is important to look at your character, the good, the bad, and the ugly of your personality. We all have things that we do well sometime, but the goal in Christian living is to do well most of the time. On the flip side of the personality coin, we all have weaknesses, or things about ourselves that need to be improved. This is a lifelong process, as we improve in one area we may fall short in another because of life's circumstances. For this part of the exercise we will look at your strengths and weaknesses.

What are your strengths?

_____

_____

_____

What are your weaknesses?

_____

_____

_____

Now it is time to compare what you think about yourself and what others think about you. Ask at least five people who know you well to describe your strengths and your weaknesses. Don't retaliate if they tell you something you do not like. Remember, this is a growth experience. Compare what you believe about yourself with the feedback you received from others.

_____

_____

_____

Do you have some strengths that you are not aware of? Describe

_____

_____

To improve your self-esteem focus on your strengths.

What are you going to do about your weaknesses?

_____

_____

_____

Now that you have taken the time to look at this part of yourself, what have you learned about your character?

_____

_____

In what areas do you need improvement?

_____

_____

Changing your life to reflect the God in you starts with a decision to make a positive change. You have taken time to look at your weaknesses which include sin and rebellion. You have probably discovered that your weaknesses consist of old baggage, which are issues in your life that remain unresolved.

Unresolved issues can be divided into two categories; those that can be resolved and those that cannot. Issues that can be resolved typically involve paying back money owed, apologizing for past deeds, and ending family feuds.

Typical unresolved issues that tend to cause guilt and shame are missing the birth of a child, missing a funeral, or not resolving issues with someone before they passed away. For these types of issues a Dear God letter is in order to give you a chance to tell your side of the story, forgive yourself, and to ask the Lord to take away your guilt and shame.

Before you proceed in contacting the person you have a grievance with make sure that you pray about it and ask the Lord for clarity, instruction, and words of wisdom. Write down what you need to discuss and get your thoughts organized. Once you have contacted them state your case in a precise and cordial manner and ask for forgiveness. Don't get angry if they do not forgive you. Bless them, pray for them, and move on to Step Four.

You have taken the first hard look at yourself. Do not be ashamed of what you have uncovered or what you have done in the past. The purpose of this step is to bring to your conscious awareness your sinful attitudes and behaviors for correction with help from the almighty God through his Word.

All scripture is given by inspiration of God, and is profitable for doctrine, for reproof, for correction, for instruction in righteousness (2 Timothy 3:16).

Say this prayer:

I acknowledged my sin unto thee, and mine iniquity have I not hid. I said I will confess my transgression unto the Lord and thou forgavest the iniquity of my sin. Selah (Psalm 32:5). Have mercy upon me O God, according to thy loving kindness, according unto the multitude of thy tender mercies blot out my transgressions. Wash me thoroughly from mine iniquity and cleanse me from my sin (Psalm 51:1-2).

STEP FOUR

FORGIVE THOSE WHO HAVE TRESPASSED AGAINST YOU

S tep Four is a step in which you learn how to let go of the past. Forgiveness is a process of acknowledging what was done that offended you and the decision to move out of offense and into the fullness of God.

Make a list of people who have sinned against you or offended you to such a degree that you have not forgiven them.

PERSON   **OFFENCE**

_____

_____

_____

It is time to look at the past issues that have kept you stuck and have prevented you from moving forward. Tragic events have a way of effecting every aspect of your life if not dealt with properly. This is the time when you need to uncover everything that you have kept buried and have refused to acknowledge or to admit that it is even bothering you.

In chronological order list your tragic life events. If you become overwhelmed take a break and read one of the prayers in Appendix A.

YEAR   **TRAGIC EVENT**

_____

_____

_____

Is there a pattern to the types of tragedies you have experienced in your life? Explain:

_____

_____

Now it is time for you to write your autobiography. As you have probably already experienced, your friends and family get tired of hearing you complain. They don't understand why you cannot get over your past. This is the time to pour out your soul to the Most High God. He will understand. He will be patient and listen to you no matter how long it takes, no matter how long you cry. Allow yourself to experience the emotions, write the unspoken words that got stuck in your throat in times past. Don't edit your thoughts or feelings. Write them as they come to you. As I said before, your story is not for publication it is for purification.

Many of you refuse to write because when you were a child a sibling or a parent found your journal and read your most intimate thoughts. As an adult, that excuse no longer holds water because you control who has access to your personal items. This is an intricate and necessary part of the healing process, do not skip it.

You have already laid the ground work by completing the exercises in steps 1—3. Incorporate into the story the people who have offended you, your sins or rebellious nature, as well as your tragic life events. This is a lengthy process, be thorough and include the good times as well. If you become overwhelmed while writing, pause and read a prayer or scripture. Do not begin the next section until you have finished this assignment.

> *Therefore my beloved brethren be ye steadfast, unmovable, always abounding in the work of the Lord, for as much as ye know that your labor is not in vain in the Lord (I Corinthians 15:58).*

The Rest Stop

Congratulations! You have completed the most difficult tasks of your journey on the road to recovery. It is time to let the Holy Spirit heal you and transform you and fill you with His glory as you forgive those who have trespassed against you. *But if you do not forgive, neither will your Father which is in heaven forgive your trespasses (Mark 11:26).*

Forgiveness

Forgiveness means to stop feeling angry or resentful toward someone for an offense, flaw, or mistake. It also means to cancel something such as a debt (Webster, 1998).

Forgiving someone does not mean that you condone their behavior or that they should not be punished for their crime. It means that you are letting go of resentment, anger, and feelings of victimization. It means you will let go of the past and live in the present with love and gratitude, thanking the Lord for another day and everything He has done for you.

It is time for you to ask the Lord to forgive you for harboring unforgiveness in your heart. Pray the following prayer out loud:

In the name of Jesus, I repent for holding grudges, and not forgiving those who have offended me. I *know that the Son of man hath power on earth to forgive sins (Matthew 9:6).* It is written that *If we confess our sins, he is faithful and just to forgive us our sins, and to cleanse us from all unrighteousness (I John 1:9).* Lord I am asking you to *look upon mine affliction and my pain and forgive all my sins (Psalm 25:18).* In Jesus' Name I pray. Amen.

What issues remain unresolved? Now it is time for you to forgive others. List the names of the people you have not forgiven and then pray out loud because there is power in the spoken word.

Prayer of Forgiveness

The Bible says to *be kind one to another, tender hearted, forgiving one another, even as God for Christ's sake hath forgiven you (Ephesians 4:32)*. In the name of Jesus I forgive (names). Lord I pray that *all bitterness, wrath, anger, clamour, and evil speaking be put away from me (Ephesians 4:31)*. From this day forward *I will love my neighbor as myself (Romans 13:9)*. The word says that *He who loveth God loveth his brother also (I John 4:21)*. *If we love one another, God dwelleth in us, and his love is perfected in us (I John 4:12)*. *God is love and he that dwelleth in love dwelleth in God (I John 4:16)*. And to those I have forgiven, I pray that they *know the love of Christ and that they may be filled with all the fullness of God (Ephesians 3:19)*. In Jesus' name I pray. Amen.

Don't Worry Be Happy

Worry means to give way to anxiety or unease and allow one's mind to dwell on difficulty or trouble (Webster, 1998). It has been my experience that people who worry all of the time are trying to control every aspect of their life and/or trying to prevent bad things from happening. They constantly think about the what-ifs of life and feel out of control and worried about what to do next.

Here is an effective way to manage your worry. Every morning put your worries on a slip of paper and put it in your God box. I use sticky notes or index cards. Schedule your worry time for an hour a day. For instance, your worry time may be scheduled from 7:00 p.m. to 8:00 p.m. daily. During the day when all the cares of the world try to take over, talk back to them and tell them- not yet! Then repeat a Bible verse to combat the worries as you stand on the Word of God such as Philippians

4:6-7, Luke 12:22-26, or Psalm 55:22. There are many Bible verses that will help you stop worrying, use the ones of your choosing.

The next step is to write about your worries during your designated time. This is also a good time to journal. In a few short weeks you will notice that worries no longer consume your day and eventually you will not need a full hour to devote to worrying. In fact, you will begin to resent it and the way you have allowed it to steal your joy.

Spiritual Exercise

Try laughing at least seven times throughout your day for fifteen to thirty seconds at a time. You will notice an improvement in your mood in less than twenty four hours. Some of you are asking when and where this is possible because of your hectic work schedule. There is actually plenty of time, as soon as you wake up, before you go to bed, while you are driving, walking to and from the parking lot, in the elevator, in the restroom, etc. It doesn't have to be a boisterous laugh, a chuckle under your breath will suffice especially in the work environment.

Keep some clean humorous material on your computer, down load jokes, pod cast, etc. that will brighten your day and make you laugh. It is my belief, that even forcing yourself to laugh will stimulate those neuro-hormones that are responsible for elevating your mood (Smith, Kemp, & Segal, 2012).

A merry heart doeth good like a medicine, but a broken spirit drieth the bones (Proverbs 17:22).

When will you laugh? Schedule it now in the space provided or in your personal calendar.

Time   Where

_____

_____

_____

_____

A New Heart

Now that you have learned to manage your worry and have forgiven those in your life who have caused you physical or emotional pain it is time for God to give you a new heart and to fill it with joy and gladness. Take a moment and ask the Lord to renew your heart. Say this out loud. *Create in me a clean heart, O God, and renew a right spirit within me (Psalm 51:10).* (Pause).

God has answered you in the following verses. *For if our heart condemn us, God is greater than our heart, and knoweth all things (I John 3:20). Then will I (God) sprinkle clean water upon you and ye shall be clean from all your filthiness, and from all your idols, will I cleanse you. A new heart also will I give you, and a new spirit will I put within you and I will take away the stony heart out of your flesh, and I will give you an heart of flesh. And I will put my spirit within you, and cause you to walk in my statutes and ye shall keep my judgments and do them (Ezekiel 36:25-27). And your heart shall rejoice and your joy no man taketh from you (John 16:22b).*

Meditate on this word from the Lord. Write down what He has spoken to you.

STEP FIVE

PRAY WITHOUT CEASING

P rayer is a powerful weapon. The Bible says to *pray without ceasing (1 Thessalonians 5:17)*. Some of you are perplexed about the logistics of that verse. What the Lord is saying is to pray every day and pray about everything. That is, converse with the Lord. Ask his advice and pray for other people. It may only be a thirty second prayer three times per day, every day. That is an example of praying without ceasing.

Your human spirit can also pray without those prayers reaching the conscious mind. Those individuals who have been called into intercessory prayer will develop a prayer life that enables them to pray without ceasing in the literal sense. Their spirit man prays continually (Goll, 2007). *And he that searcheth the hearts knoweth what is the mind of the Spirit, because he maketh intercession for the saints according to the will of God (Romans 8:26-27).*

HOW TO PRAY

Pray For Your Enemies

We have all been hurt by other people at some time in our lives. The only way to defeat them and forgive them is to use God's principles, love and prayer.

> *But I say unto you, love your enemies, bless them that curse you, do good to them that hate you, and pray for them which despitefully use you, and persecute you (Matthew 5:44).*

Pray From The Heart And With Sincerity

It is important not to get into legalism, praying because you think you have to. Ask God to change your heart and transform your mind so that you can pray the will of the Father with sincerity.

When thou prayest, enter into thy closet and when thou hast shut thy door, pray to thy Father which is in secret, and thy Father which seeth in secret shall reward thee openly. But when you pray, use not vain repetitions as the heathen do, for they think that they shall be heard for their much speaking (Matthew 6:6-7).

Perhaps you have not prayed regularly and you are unsure of what to say. Pray the Lord's Prayer as the Spirit leads.

The Lord's Prayer

Our Father which art in heaven, hallowed be thy name. Thy Kingdom come, Thy will be done in earth as it is in heaven. Give us this day our daily bread. And forgive us our debts as we forgive our debtors. And lead us not into temptation, but deliver us from evil. For thine is the kingdom, and the power, and the glory, forever. Amen (Matthew 6:9-13).

Pray In The Spirit or In Tongues

For if I pray in an unknown tongue my spirit prayeth, but my understanding is unfruitful. I will pray with the spirit and I will pray with the understanding (I Corinthians 14:14-15). This is a powerful tool in your arsenal to defeat the powers of darkness. As you pray in tongues your human spirit converses with the spirit of God in a heavenly language. You may not know what you are praying but God knows and your spirit knows. This is the perfect prayer.

Baptized In The Holy Spirit

In order to speak in tongues you must be baptized in the Holy Spirit. Most of you will not speak in the interpretation of tongues and it is not necessary in order to use this tool that the Lord has provided for us. If you would like to receive the baptism of the Holy Spirit with evidence of speaking in tongues pray the following:

Dear Heavenly Father, your words says that *how much more shall your heavenly Father give the Holy Spirit to them that ask Him? (Luke 11:13b)*. In the name of Jesus I am asking you to fill me with your Holy Spirit with the evidence of speaking in tongues according to Acts 1:8, 2:4). It is written that *the prophecy came not in old time by the will of man, but holy men of God spake as they were moved by the Holy Ghost (2 Peter 1:21). And our gospel came not unto you in word only, but also in power and in the Holy Ghost (I Thessalonians 1:5).* Therefore heavenly Father I will speak with other tongues as the Spirit gives me utterance (Acts 2:4) to pray for others and to fight the power of darkness. In Jesus' name I pray. Amen.

Now just open your mouth and let the Spirit of the Most High God guide your speech. Do not be afraid it will become as comfortable as your natural language in due time. Some of you will sing in tongues, just let it flow and do not hold back. If you are unsure about what you are hearing call a spirit-filled friend and have them pray with you. It is as simple as that.

Intercession

Intercession is defined as prayer or petition in favor of another (Goll, 2007). The Holy Spirit intercedes for us, Jesus intercedes for us, and we are to intercede for each other. Praying in tongues means praying in the Spirit. For those of you who have been baptized in the Holy Spirit, pray in tongues when you don't know what to pray. Again I reiterate, it is the perfect prayer.

Likewise the Spirit also helpeth our infirmities, for we know not what we should pray for as we ought, but the Spirit itself maketh intercession for us with groanings which cannot be uttered. And he that searcheth the hearts knoweth what is the mind of the Spirit, because he maketh intercession for the saints according to the will of God (Romans8:26-27).

It is Christ that died, yea rather, that is risen again, who is even at the right hand of God, who also maketh intercession for us (Romans 10:34).

Confess your faults one to another, and pray one for another, that ye may be healed. The effectual fervent prayer of a righteous man availeth much (James 5:16).

Prophetic Intercession

Prophetic Intercession is prayer that is directed by the Holy Spirit. It is prophetic because the request comes from God and the individual praying has little or no knowledge of the circumstances. *And he that searcheth the hearts knoweth what is the mind of the Spirit, because he maketh intercession for the saints according to the will of God (Romans 8:27).* In prophetic intercession, the Holy Spirit directs the individual to pray for a particular person or situation. When God has a burden on his heart, He shares it with the intercessor so that the intercessor can pray the burden back to God with moaning and groaning. In this way the Holy Spirit can intervene on the earth to change the situation through prayers (Goll, 2007). The prophetic intercessor will travail in the spirit until God's purpose is birthed on the earth. *For we know not what we should pray for as we ought, but the Spirit itself maketh intercession for us with groanings which cannot be uttered (Romans 8:26). For we know that the whole creation groaneth and travaileth in pain together until now (Romans 8:22).*

Now that you know how to pray make a commitment to prayer. For those of you who spend hours a day in your car commuting between work and home, use this time for prayer. When you run out of things to pray in your native tongue, pray in the spirit, in the unknown tongue.

List the people you will pray for:

_____

_____

When will you pray and how will you pray?

_____

_____

What is the Lord speaking to your heart right now?

_____

_____

_____

STEP SIX

DELIVERANCE FROM STRONGHOLDS

S trongholds are the issues you are struggling with in your life. A stronghold is defined as a fortified place, a fortress (Webster, 1998). When you are being held in bondage and imprisoned by the forces within, it seems that no matter how hard you try, you cannot break free. Some typical strongholds are cursing, uncontrolled anger, procrastination, smoking, drinking, or some other type of addictive behavior, eating disorders, depression, anxiety, etc. List your strongholds below.

_____

_____

You are enslaved and bound by the forces that you just disclosed. In order to break free you need to be aware of your rights as a child of God. Before you pray read John 14:14, John 16:23, I John 3:8, Matthew 16:19, I Corinthians 2:16, Psalm 107:19-20.

Use the following prayer to ask the Most High God for deliverance from your strongholds. Pray this daily, several times a day if needed, until you are free. The repetition of the prayer is for you not God. This is one way to get the Word of God into your soul. The scriptures state that death and life are in the power of the tongue (Proverbs 18:21) and faith cometh by hearing, and hearing by the word of God (Romans 10:17).

Heavenly Father, I come to you in the name of Jesus. I repent for all sins I have committed knowingly and unknowingly and I ask you to cleanse me of all unrighteousness. Your word says that if I shall ask anything in your name you shall do it. Therefore, heavenly Father I ask you to deliver me from _____.

It is written that whatsoever I bind on earth shall be bound in heaven and whatsoever is loosed on earth will be loosed in heaven. Your Word says that I have the mind of Christ and that I am free from the law of sin and death. In the mighty name of Jesus I take authority over every stronghold that is affecting my mind, body and spirit. I bind it and cast it to the feet of Jesus never to return to me again. I bind every obsessive thought, compulsive behavior, and negative attitude. Lord you said in the scripture that, He sent His word and healed me and delivered me from my destruction. And for that Lord I thank you and I receive it, in Jesus' name I pray. Amen.

Many strongholds run in families and are passed down from one generation to the next. Think about your extended family. What issues do they struggle with? Is there a pattern? For example; is there a history of suicide, infertility, incarceration, or a pattern of early death among the men in your family? List the strongholds below.

If several family members suffer from the same affliction this is actually a generational curse. You can pray against it and break the power of the curse by using the name and the blood of Jesus. Read the following verses before you pray so that you have an understanding of what you are praying. Psalm 79:8, Psalm 91, I Peter 1:19, Ephesians 1:7, 6:12, Hebrews 9:22, and Revelations 12:11. Now read through the prayer and fill in the blanks as instructed. Once that is completed read the prayer out loud with boldness.

Prayer For Breaking Generational Curses

Father in the name of Jesus, I repent for my sins and those sins committed by my ancestors for at least four generations. Lord through your crucifixion you were made a living sacrifice. You shed your blood for us as a lamb without blemish or spot. It is written in your word that almost all things are by the law purged with blood and through Christ. We have redemption through your blood, and the forgiveness of sins. In the name of Jesus Christ and by the power of your shed blood I take authority over every generational curse in my mother's *bloodline and my father's bloodline the (family names)* In the name of Jesus, I bind every spirit of (generational curses) In the name of Jesus, I denounce and bind all works of Satan that entered into our family through the practices of witchcraft, sorcery, covens, spells, hexes, curses, vexes, palm and tarot card readings, idolatry, false religions, ungodly soul ties, ungodly social organizations, pornography, and every ungodly sin that was practiced or spoken by my family and ancestors. In the name of Jesus, I cancel and nullify every spirit of death that has been assigned to our families the (names) and I ask the Lord Jesus to sprinkle His blood over us and to send ministering angels to surround and protect us. For we wrestle not against flesh and blood but against principalities, against powers, against the rulers of the darkness of this world. Against spiritual wickedness in high places. Heavenly Father, in the name of Jesus I ask you to fill us with your Holy Spirit. Heavenly Father I pray that my family be strengthened with might by His Spirit in their inner man. I pray that in the ages to come the Lord might show the exceeding riches of his grace in his kindness toward us through Christ Jesus. To God be the glory. Amen.*

(*If you do not know the names of your biological parents the Holy Spirit will intercede for you)

Write down how you feel and what the Lord revealed to you in this section.

If you do not belong to a Bible based church it is imperative that you find one to be under the power of the corporate anointing and to stay free from the afflictions that have kept you bound. Breaking free of strongholds and staying free is facilitated by having others pray for you, laying hands on you, anointing you with oil, or participating in a deliverance session by an anointed minister of God.

The Power Of Praying With Others

Most churches have prayer ministries or prayer teams. You can ask for prayer during a Sunday service or any time the doors to the church are open. If in doubt, ask. If no one is available to pray with you and for you then you are at the wrong church. All of the mega-churches, that have regularly televised programs have prayer lines that are available 24/7 at no cost to the caller. Turn the channel to one of the Christian stations and you will be exposed to a plethora of ministries that can serve you.

How should one chase a thousand, and two put ten thousand to flight (Deuteronomy 32:30). That if two of you shall agree on earth as touching anything that they shall ask, it shall be done for them of my Father which is in heaven. For where two or three are gathered together in my name, there I am in the midst of them (Matthew 18:19-20).

The Power of Laying On Of Hands

This should be done by the Pastors, Elders of the church, and all Christians who are the body of Christ.

And when they had prayed, they laid hands on them (Acts 6:6). Then laid they their hands on them and they received the Holy Ghost (Acts 8:17). And Joshua the son of Nun was full of the spirit of wisdom, for Moses had laid his hands upon him (Deuteronomy 8:10a). They shall lay hands on the sick and they shall recover (Mark 16:18b).

The Power of Deliverance

God has all power in heaven and earth and He will deliver you through a minister, through his Word, or through the

Holy Spirit. However He chooses to deliver you it will be a supernatural experience.

> *For thou hast delivered my soul from death, mine eyes from tears, and my feet from falling (Psalm 116:8). Surely he shall deliver thee from the snare of the fowler and from the noisome pestilence(Psalm 91:3). And now Lord, what wait I for? My hope is in thee. Deliver me from all my transgressions (Psalm 39:7-8). I trusted in thee, O Lord, I said thou art my God. My times are in thy hand, deliver me from the hand of mine enemies, and from them that persecute me (Psalm 31:14-15). Seek good and not evil that ye may live and so the Lord the God of hosts shall be with you (Amos5:14)*

Power In The Tongue

Be very careful and deliberate about what you say because there is power in the spoken word.

> *And all things whatsoever ye shall ask in prayer, believing, ye shall receive (Matthew 21:21-22). And they were filled with the Holy Ghost, and began to speak with other tongues, as the Spirit gave them utterance (Acts 2:4). Deliver my soul, O Lord, from lying lips, and from a deceitful tongue (Psalm 120:2). Death and life are in the power of the tongue, and they that love it shall eat the fruit thereof (Proverbs 18:21). If ye shall say unto this mountain, be thou removed and be thou cast into the sea it shall be done.*

The Power of Anointing Oil

Anointing oil is used as a point of contact for the Holy Spirit. You can buy the oil from other ministries but that is not necessary. You can use an oil of your choosing like olive oil or vegetable oil. However, it must be prayed over by a spirit-filled Christian. Anoint yourself before you pray, before bed, upon awakening, etc. Use the oil to anoint every window and every door in your home and office. Let the Holy Spirit direct you in this area.

Thou hast loved righteousness and hated iniquity, therefore God even thy God, hath anointed thee with the oil of gladness above thy fellows (Hebrews 1:9). I entered into a covenant with thee, saith the Lord God, and thou becamest mine. Then washed I thee with water, yea I thoroughly washed away thy blood from thee and I anointed thee with oil (Ezekiel 16:8-9).

And they cast out many devils and anointed with oil many that were sick, and healed them (Mark 6:13). Is any sick among you? Let him call for the elders of the church and let them pray over him anointing him with oil in the name of the Lord (James 5:14). Thou preparest a table before me in the presence of mine enemies, thou anointest my head with oil, my cup runneth over. Surely goodness and mercy shall follow me all the days of my life and I will dwell in the house of the Lord forever (Psalm 23:5-6).

Communion

Communion is also called the last supper. In Mark 14:12-25, Jesus eats His last supper or the Passover meal, with His twelve disciples. The elements used today are bread and wine (or grape juice) which represent His body and His blood. *And as they did eat, Jesus took bread and blessed and brake it and gave to them and said, take, eat: this is my body. And he took the cup and when he had given thanks, he gave it to them and they all drank of it. And he said unto them, this is my blood of the new testament which is shed for many (Mark 15:22-24).*

Communion is practiced differently within the body of Christ. Some denominations only serve communion twice a year, while another denomination will serve it monthly, and still others will make this part of the weekly service. Whatever the frequency, the reenactment of the last supper is full of resurrection power. We take communion to remind ourselves that Jesus died on the cross to bear our sins, and to thank Him for being the last and final sacrifice. Many Christians see this only as a symbolic representation of the Last Supper. In actuality, as we partake of the bread and the wine, we are consuming the power of the resurrection, for healing, deliverance, and to be set free from all afflictions. The Lord has instructed me to take communion every night to circumvent the attacks of the enemy, and in so doing, nothing shall by any means hurt me.

The Inner Witness

The inner witness is given to us as protection and guidance. It is available to every believer and it is not dependent on our level of spiritual development. It is the feeling one gets when one walks into a room sensing that something is wrong. It is a way of knowing what to do without any evidence or communication with others. It is a way of knowing what to do without hearing the audible voice of God. The world refers to this as a "gut feeling" but the Bible says *The spirit of man is the candle of the Lord, searching all the inward parts of the belly (Proverbs 20:27).*

Pay attention to how you feel. This is another method in which the Lord communicates. When a situation or person makes you uncomfortable, then take the opportunity to reevaluate the situation. Pray about it, talk with others about it. If the circumstance does not permit time for you to talk with others, then make a decision on the communication sent forth by the Inner Witness which is the Holy Spirit.

Describe at least two times when you were led by the inner witness.

STEP SEVEN

REBUKE THE DEVOURER

There are two types of spiritual forces operating in this world, and they are the spirits of good and evil. We live in a world that is dominated by Satan, the evil intelligence. Because of this, we as humans are subjected to the law of sin and death. Many Christians don't understand who and what they are fighting. That gives Satan the advantage. Once you understand who you are and whose you are then the victory in your life is just a matter of time. This doesn't mean you will no longer have set backs but it means that you will have more victories.

And I will rebuke the devourer for your sakes, and he shall not destroy the fruits of your ground (Malachi 3:11). At thy rebuke they fled, at the voice of thy thunder they hasted away (Psalm 104:7).

Who Is The Devourer?

The devourer is Lucifer, also called Satan, the devil, the accuser of the brethren, beelzebub, the prince of darkness, the serpent and many others. He has a well organized army comprised of demons who are bodiless, dark spirits. Demons have been on the earth from the beginning of time and they roam the earth as well as the heavenlies. They do not die a physical death because they have no body. Therefore, their greatest desire is to live in a human body by any means necessary. How do they gain entrance you ask? They gain entrance through your soul and if they can capture your soul then they can capture your body.

Demons are Lucifer's soldiers and they have been given assignments. They are on a mission to destroy every human being on the face of this planet (Sumrall, 2003) through physical or mental illness or by any method that will cause havoc and strife in your life.

But the thief cometh not, but for to steal and to kill, and to destroy (John 10:10). Be sober, be vigilant, because your adversary the devil, as a roaring lion, walketh about, seeking whom he may devour (I Peter 5:8).

Satan is a supernatural being and therefore he has supernatural power. Don't be dismayed because the Most High God has all power in heaven and in earth.

It is important to understand how the enemy works if you are to have victory in your life. Satan is the antithesis of God, he hates what God loves, he is evil. He operates through fear because he is fear. Fear is the opposite of faith. If you are in fear, you are worried, not feeling in control, and are most likely looking to mortal women and men to solve your problems. Your eyes are not on God when you are in fear. This allows doubt and confusion to creep in. This is a tactic that Satan uses to keep the people of God from experiencing the fullness of God, by keeping us in fear.

We all become afraid at times. I am not talking about the type of fear one experiences when the house is on fire or while being approached by a barking pit bull. Of course, that type of fear is natural and you can combat those types of situations by putting on the full armor of God and pleading the blood of Jesus. At other times, you may begin to feel that sense of doom and gloom, or worry and fear about the "what ifs" of life. Don't accept the lies of the enemy. Cast down those imaginations and rebuke the devourer in Jesus' name.

Casting down imaginations, and every high thing that exalteth itself against the knowledge of God, and bringing into captivity every thought to the obedience of Christ (2 Corinthians 10:5).

Who Are You?

As discussed previously, God is a triune God. God the Father, God the Son, and God the Holy Spirit. We were created in God's image as triune beings with a body, soul, and spirit. Your physical body houses your soul and spirit. The soul is comprised of your mind, which is your intellect, your will, and emotions. The human spirit is connected to and communicates with God's Spirit (Hormann, 1985).

Once you are born again you become a new creature in Christ. You are in the world but you are not of the world. *They are not of the world, even as I am not of the world. Sanctify them through thy truth, thy word is truth (John 17:16-17).* That is, you must change your way of thinking and behaving and live according to the Kingdom of God not according to the ideals and mores of this world. *In Him we live and move have our being (Acts 17:28).* Live in Him, walk in Him, and breathe in Him so saith the spirit of the Most High God.

How Does The Devourer Gain Access?

Demons gain access to your body by various methods. We are all susceptible because we live in this world. More specifically demons gain access through permission, deception, curses, sin, and fear. If you have been involved in a cult, coven, chanted, cast spells, participated in séance's, tarot card or palm readings, used Ouija boards, or were dedicated to Satan as a child, then the devil and his cohorts were given permission to attach themselves to you (MacNutt, 1995).

Regard not them that have familiar spirits, neither seek after wizards, to be defiled by them, I am the Lord your God (Leviticus 19:31).

Satan is very crafty, after all he is the father of lies. If you don't adhere to his doctrine he has devised other ways to get his tentacles into you. He will deceive you by causing doubt about who you are and about who Jesus is. Over the years I have observed that the media of movies, books, magazines, and television are replete with Anti-Christ messages. Many of these messages are subliminal, that is they are below our level of conscious awareness. The following is a brief list of anti-Christ messages that are in many of the above venues that are shown to be fun and unusual without detrimental consequences. That is the deception. In the end Satan is never fun and he always leaves you worse off than you were before you fell into his web of deception.

Shape Shifting - the ability to turns oneself into an animal at will

Glamorization of vampires, werewolves, and psychics (mediums)

Astral Projection - through meditation the ability to have one's soul leave your body to travel through time and distance.

Reincarnation - many lives after death returning as humans or animals

Levitation - the ability to supernaturally lift your self or objects without using a physical force that defies the law of gravity.

Talking to the dead - through séances, spirit guides, crystal balls, or mediums. These spirits are actually familiar spirits or demons.

If you have small children screen what they watch, read, and listen to. Many of the cartoon super heroes call on the power of darkness to obtain super human strength. From now on, use the mind of Christ and your inner witness as you entertain yourself through print media, television, movies, and video games.

Another pitfall to allowing demonic attack is through sin, physical contact, and objects. Committing acts of sin like gambling, using drugs, pornography, committing adultery, etc. will give evil spirits access to your soul, it is a legal opening. Evil spirits can also be transferred through sexual contact, or physical contact that is not sexual in nature. Evil spirits have the ability to attach themselves to objects. Look around your home and office. Do you have masks and trinkets that you bought on vacation that you are unsure of their origin or what they represent? If so remove them and the atmosphere in your home or office will change for the better.

Tattoos and body piercings may be legal openings as well. *Ye shall not make any cuttings in your flesh for the dead, nor print any marks upon you. I am the Lord (Leviticus 19:28).* Be careful who you allow to touch you and what is imprinted on your body. As a born again believer you are now a vessel for the Holy Spirit. *For he is a chosen vessel unto me, to bear my name, before the Gentiles and kings (Acts 9:15).*

Another avenue in which demonic oppression happens is when a person becomes severely fearful or traumatized. Through no fault of their own, these events open the soul without the person's consent. For example; victims of natural disasters, car accidents, near fatal drowning, seeing someone killed or severely injured, having been physically or sexually abused may lead to extreme fear which leads to an open soul. Watching a horror film or reading a book of the same nature may have the same effect on your soul (MacNutt, 1995). When these events happen it is helpful to receive Godly counseling so that you are able to work through your issues and overcome the power of darkness that has engulfed your soul.

Signs Of Demonic Activity

There are many ways that demons make themselves known. Sometimes they cause furniture or objects to move across the room or they cause objects to appear or disappear during séances or other occult practices. Some individuals have reported olfactory, auditory, and visual hallucinations. That is smelling, hearing, and/or seeing things that are not in this realm of existence. Theses sensations usually produce fear, torment, and other feelings of uneasiness. If this is happening in your home or office rebuke it in the name of Jesus. This is nothing to play with. Do not ask them to show themselves or reveal themselves to you. Doing so gives them permission to come into this realm of existence. This is not your spirit guide! Do not be deceived, demons are not your friends!

If this happens only while you are intoxicated then that is the answer, STOP USING!

How To Evict Them

Rebuke them in the Name of Jesus and use Steps Two and Six.

Believe in the Lord and use His name. *That at the name of Jesus every knee should bow of things in heaven, and things in earth, and things under the earth (Philippians 2:10).* The name above every name is Jesus. Jesus will heal, deliver, and set free. *He that believeth and is baptized shall be saved; but he that believeth not shall be damned. And these signs shall follow them that believe. In my name shall they cast out devils, they shall speak with new tongues. They shall take up serpents and if they drink any deadly thing, it shall not hurt them, they shall lay hands on the sick and they shall recover (Mark 16: 16-18).*

Every Christian has been given the authority over the devil. *Behold, I give unto you power to tread on serpents and scorpions, and* over all the power of the enemy; and nothing shall by any means hurt you (Luke 10:19).

Another weapon to use against Satan is the Holy Spirit and prayer. Acts 1:5, 8 reads *but ye shall be baptized with the Holy Ghost, but ye shall receive power after that the Holy Ghost is come upon you.* Pray Psalm 91 and Ephesians 6:10-19 for protection against the enemy. Pray in the spirit which is praying in tongues.

Make the demons uncomfortable. Stay in the word of God. *For the word of God is quick and powerful and sharper than any two edged sword, piercing even to the dividing asunder of soul and spirit, and of the joints and marrow, and is a discerner of the thoughts and intents of the heart (Hebrews 4:12).* Plead the blood of Jesus over yourself, family, possessions, and home. *And they overcame him by the blood of the lamb and by the word of their testimony (Revelation 12:11). In whom we have redemption through his blood, the forgiveness of sins, according to the riches of his grace (Ephesians 1:7).* Load up your heavenly arsenal, put on the full armor of God so that you will be victorious in your battles against the enemy.

Warfare And Protection Prayers

Now that you know what you are fighting it is suggested that you read Psalm 91 and Ephesians 6:10-19 daily. Personalize the scriptures by changing the pronouns to the first person.

What have you learned about the power of God?

_____

_____

What have you learned about the power of God in the believer?

_____

_____

What tools are you going to use to defeat the power of darkness?

_____

_____

If you continue to be tormented, then it will be necessary to go through a deliverance session. Unfortunately you cannot deliver yourself. You can ask God to deliver you without human intervention. If that does not happen you will need to be delivered by a spirit filled Christian, someone with experience in the deliverance ministry. It may take more than one deliverance session but do not be dismayed, this is quite common. If you do not want to be delivered you have given the demons permission to stay. That is also quite common because many people do not want to give up their sinful ways (Hammond, 2004). If you want to get free let the Lord lead you to a spirit filled church where the gifts of the spirit are in operation. Submit yourselves to God, resist the devil and he will flee from you (James 4:7).

(How to submit to God is explained in Step 8).

Salvation Is Free But The Works of Darkness Will Cost You Everything

The Lord has revealed that many of you are reading this book out of curiosity and are not born again Christians and therefore you have not answered the questions or read the scriptures. Many of you do not believe in the spirit realm and while others believe in the spirit realm, you do not believe in the devil. Some of you were attracted to the occult because of its promise of supernatural power.

In the days to come, think about the answers to the following questions. If you are unable to answer a question come back to it later, sometimes the answers are buried deep within your soul. Thoroughly explain or describe your responses to the questions in your journal or in the space provided. Don't just answer yes or no. Explain why you hold a particular belief or do things a certain way. Allow the unconscious to become conscious. Give yourself permission to remember.

God, Science, and Religion

Do you believe in God?
Do you believe in Jesus?
How did you arrive at these beliefs?
Did something happen in your life that made you turn away from God?
Are you angry at God?
Do you have a calling on your life?
Has a man or woman of God prophesied over your life and if so what did they say?
Are you running from God?
Do you dislike organized religion?
Is your belief system driven by science? If so if you were born 200 years ago how would science have effected your belief system?
If you did believe in God, how would your life change?

Supernatural Experiences

How old were you when you had your first supernatural experience, i.e., seeing ghost, having an imaginary friend, hearing things that others cannot hear?
Have you ever had an out of body experience?
Do you practice astral projection and if so what do experience before, during, and after?
Have you ever had a life after death experience?
Have you ever had a "hell" dream or experience?

Do you believe in Satan or demons and how did you arrive at these beliefs?

Family, Friends, and Other Things

Do other people complain about your behavior or attitude?
Do you have trouble keeping jobs or making friends?
Are others afraid of you at times and if so why?
What kind of music, television, movies, video games, books do you like and is there a common theme?
What is your sexual orientation?

Fear

In life, what are you most afraid of?
Are you afraid to be alone? If so, why?
Do you ever feel unreal, or detached from your body?
Do you have nightmares on a regular basis or recurring dreams? If so describe them and is there a common theme?
Do you suffer from insomnia, night terrors or sleep walking?
Do you speak with different voices that are not your own during sleep or wake?
Do you suffer from black outs, that is not remembering what you did for a period of time? When do they occur, what is their frequency, and are they drug or alcohol induced?

Hindrances to Receiving the Fullness of God

Do you cut on yourself or mutilate your body in any way?
Do you have more tattoos and body piercings than the average person?
Are you still suffering from being verbally, physically, or sexually abused?

Have you done something that you think is so horrible that you do not believe that God will forgive you?

Death

Have you or your partner ever conceived a child that ended in abortion?
Have you ever had suicidal thoughts or tried to commit suicide?
Have you ever had homicidal thoughts or tried to or committed homicide?
If you died tomorrow where would you spend eternity? Are you sure?

Are you ready to be free from pain and torment? If so, start reading this book again, beginning with Step One. No longer read this book out of curiosity but read it as a means to be delivered from your tragic life events. Answer the questions and read the scriptures so that the Lord, the most High God can set you free. Some of you will need to seek professional help from clergy, therapists, medical staff, or attorneys because of your unresolved issues. God has put His people in every profession. Do not be afraid to ask for help. This is the way of the Lord in this hour.

The Lord has already revealed Himself to some of you. Feel the warmth of the Holy Spirit and bask in His glory. If you are ready to commit to the Lord read the *Prayer of Salvation* in Step Two.

STEP EIGHT

SUBMIT TO GOD

The Lord is everything you need Him to be if you allow it. God's ways are not your ways. The Most High God, the creator of this universe has all power in heaven and in earth. He has given us power through the gifts of the Holy Spirit. Submit yourself to Him only and allow God to open up your gifts that have laid dormant.

Submit yourselves therefore to God. Resist the devil, and he will flee from you (James 4:7).

Gifts Of The Holy Spirit

God the Father has power and He wants to give us power to defeat the enemy. These gifts are administered by the third person of the trinity, the Holy Spirit. These gifts are not for us, but they function through us, for the uplifting of the body of Christ (Sumrall, 1982). There are nine gifts of the spirit as given to us in I Corinthians 12:8-10. *For to one is given by the Spirit the word of wisdom, to another the word of knowledge by the same spirit. To another faith by the same Spirit, to another the gifts of healing by the same Spirit. To another the working of miracles, to another prophecy, to another discerning of spirits, to another divers kinds of tongues, to another the interpretation of tongues.*

The nine gifts can be divided into three categories, the revelation gifts, the power gifts, and the inspiration gifts. God has made these gifts available to the body of Christ (Sumrall, 1982). However, just like any gift, they must be given and accepted.

Revelation Gifts

The revelation gifts consist of the gift of the word of wisdom, the gift of the word of knowledge, and the gift of discerning of spirits (Sumrall, 1982).

The gift of the word of wisdom is given supernaturally by the Holy Spirit. *The God of our Lord Jesus Christ, the Father of glory, may give unto you the spirit of wisdom and revelation in the knowledge of him (Ephesians 1:17).* It is a small fragment of God's wisdom that is given to an individual as a way to counsel, advise (Price, 2006) or warn of danger. *But the wisdom that is from above is first pure, then peaceable, gentle, and easy to be entreated (James 3:17).* In the Old Testament every seer (prophet) had the gift of the word of wisdom (Sumrall, 1982). Moses and Solomon were given wisdom to lead and make decisions.

The gift of the word of knowledge are facts supernaturally revealed by the Holy Spirit to an individual about others. Typically, the Holy Spirit reveals information about someone's health, conduct, or spiritual attitude. The difference between the word of wisdom and the word of knowledge is that the word of wisdom will help us make choices and guides others. The word of knowledge reveals things about people or situations that already exist (Sumrall, 1982).

An example of this is written in I Samuel 10. In these scriptures Samuel told Saul where to find the lost donkeys as revealed to him by the Holy Spirit. *When you have departed from me today, you will find two men by Rachel's tomb in the territory of Benjamin at Zelzah. And they will say to you, The donkeys which you went to look for have been found (I Samuel 10:2 NKJ).*

The gift of discerning of spirits is given by the Holy Spirit to help us understand what is influencing a person's behavior. This gift will discern if the behavior is of the Holy Spirit, the human spirit, or an evil spirit (MacNutt, 1995). *And it came to pass as we went to prayer, a certain damsel possessed with a spirit of divination met us, which brought her masters much gain by soothsaying. And this did she many days. But Paul, being grieved turned and said to the spirit, I command thee in the name of Jesus Christ to come out of her. And he came out the same hour (Acts 16:16, 18).* In this scripture, Paul discerned what type of spirit was operating and he cast it out in the name of Jesus. This gift is very helpful for those of us in the deliverance ministry.

Power Gifts

The power gifts are the gift of faith, the gift of healing, and the working of miracles. With the gift of faith no human effort is needed as God brings about a supernatural change into this realm of existence (Sumrall, 1982). The Christian must believe that it is so and wait for the manifestation of what he/she is believing for. *So then faith cometh by hearing and hearing by the word of God (Romans 10:17). And Jesus answering saith unto them, Have faith in God. Therefore I say unto you, what things so ever ye desire, when ye pray, believe that ye receive them, and ye shall have them (Mark 11:22, 24).*

The gift of healing is supernaturally given by the Holy Spirit to individuals so that they may pray for other people who suffer from various diseases and conditions (Sumrall, 1982). God does the healing as He works through the anointed minister as an instrument to heal those afflicted. *And it came to pass that the father of Publius lay sick of a fever and of a bloody flux to whom Paul entered in and prayed, and laid his hands on him, and healed him (Acts 28:8).*

The working of miracles are events and achievements that are not limited to the laws of the natural world (Price, 2006). For example people being raised from the dead, the blind seeing, missing or damaged body parts being restored are truly miracles. Jesus raised Lazarus from the dead by commanding it. *Said I not unto thee that if thou wouldest believe thou shouldest see the glory of God? And Jesus lifted up his eyes and said, Father I thank thee that thou has heard me. And when he thus had spoken he cried with a loud voice, Lazarus come forth. And he that was dead came forth, bound hand and foot with graveclothes (John 11:40-44).*

In the book of Acts, the Apostle Peter brought healing to a lame man by commanding him to walk in the name of Jesus. *In the name of Jesus Christ of Nazareth rise up and walk. And he took him by the right hand and lifted him up and immediately his feet and ankle bones received strength. And he leaping up stood and walked and entered with them into the temple walking, and leaping, and praising God (Acts 3:6-8).*

The most High God, the Father of Glory is speaking to you now. Even though you may be in the midst of a trying time the Lord wants you to stand on His Word. *Rejoicing in hope, patient in tribulation, continuing instant in prayer (Romans 12:12)* because *I (Jesus) give unto you power to tread on serpents and scorpions, and over all the power of the enemy and nothing shall by any means hurt you (Luke 10:19).* Give Him all of your burdens, all of your pain, and all of your fear. The Spirit of the Lord is commanding you to rise up and leap with joy. *Rejoice ye in that day and leap for joy, for behold your reward is great in heaven (Luke 6:23). Rejoice in the Lord always, and again I say, rejoice (Philippians 4:4).*

What did the Lord just reveal to you?

Inspiration Gifts

The inspiration gifts are the gift of prophecy, the gift of tongues, and the gift of the interpretation of tongues (Sumrall, 1982). *Wherefore brethren, covet to prophesy, and forbid not to speak with tongues (I Corinthians 14:39).* These gifts are for personal worship and for corporate worship, for the edifying of the church (Hamon, 2008).

The gift of prophecy is inspired communication from Father God. This supernatural communication has three spiritual levels consisting of the spirit of prophecy, the gift of prophecy, and the office of the prophet. The Spirit of Prophecy is an atmosphere created by the Holy Spirit so that all believers can yield to the Spirit of Prophesy to speak about the goodness of

Jesus. *Let us prophesy according to the proportion of faith (Romans 12:6). For we know in part and we prophesy in part (I Corinthians 13:9).* It is an anointing that comes out of the believer when the Spirit of Prophecy is present. Any believer can enter into the anointing and prophesy (Hamon, 2008).

The Gift of Prophecy is the second level of the prophetic realm. It is received by faith and cannot be earned (Hamon, 2008). The gift of prophecy never predicts the future but is used for edification, exhortation, and comfort (Sumrall, 1982). *But he that prophesieth speaketh unto men to edification, and exhortation, and comfort (I Corinthians 14:3).*

The Office of the Prophet is the third level of the prophetic realm. God uses men and women of God to speak words that are used for correction, comfort, exhortation, edification, and prediction (Sumrall, 1982). The office of the prophet is one of the five-fold ministry gifts given to the church as explained in Ephesians 4:11-12.

And he gave some apostles, and some prophets, and some evangelists and some pastors and teachers. For the perfecting of the saints for the work of the ministry, for the edifying of the body of Christ. The Office of The Prophet is a headship ministry. God uses prophets to impart and stir up spiritual gifts, to decree God's judgments and blessings, and to anoint ministries (Hamon, 2008).

In the Bible there are several prophets in the Old and New Testaments. There are twelve minor prophets categorized as such because their writings were small as compared to the major prophets. The minor prophets are Hosea, Joel, Amos, Obadiah, Jonah, Micah, Nahum, Habakkuk, Zephaniah, Haggai, Zechriah, and Malachi. The major prophets are identified as Isaiah, Ezekiel, Jeremiah, and Daniel. These prophets are located in the Old Testament and there are many prophets in the New Testament. Jesus and his apostles were prophets as well as Anna and Miriam (Price, 2006). Now that you know who they are, read about them in the Bible for clarity, revelation knowledge, and a more in depth study.

The gift of tongues is one of the most misunderstood gifts within the body of Christ. Some denominations forbid their members to speak in tongues without an interpreter, while other Christians believe that speaking in tongues is from the enemy. Satan has distorted many of God's gifts to cause confusion among believers and non-believers as well. In actuality the gift of tongues is a message given from God, through the Holy Spirit in an unknown tongue or language. It is your spirit talking to the Holy Spirit in a language the devil does not understand.

Speaking in tongues is a multi-faceted gift that has been explained throughout the New Testament. The following verses will give clarity to the purpose of the gift of tongues.

The gift of tongues is used for edifying yourself. *He that speaketh in an unknown tongue edifieth himself (I Corinthians 14;14).*

The gift of tongues is used to magnify God. *They heard them speak with tongues and magnify God (Acts 10:46).*

The gift of tongues is used as intercessory prayer. *Likewise the Spirit also helpeth our infirmities for we know not what we should pray for as we ought, but the Spirit itself maketh intercession for us with groanings which cannot be uttered (Romans 8:26).*

The gift of tongues is used in singing. *I will sing with the spirit and I will sing with the understanding also (I Corinthians 14:15).*

The interpretation of tongues is the third gift of inspiration. The person speaking in tongues has no knowledge of what he/she is saying (Sumrall, 1982). The Bible says that a person with the gift of tongues should seek interpretation of the gift as written in I Corinthians 14:13. *Wherefore let him that speaketh in an unknown tongue pray that he interpret.* A person with this gift will interpret what was spoken by another in an unknown or heavenly tongue. The interpretation is not an exact grammatical translation. The Holy Spirit will give the individual the interpretation to make known what God is saying (Sumrall, 1982).

What gifts do you already possess? What gifts are you praying for?

_____

_____

Covenant Promises

Covenant promises are given to the citizens of the Kingdom of God. In order to understand what God has promised we must first understand what a covenant is and we must understand the covenants that God made with us. The Bible is a book of covenants and a covenant is defined as a formal and binding agreement (Webster, 1998).

In some ancient civilizations covenants were based on differences not similarities. The purpose of the union was to share resources, goods, or abilities that the other family did not possess. The covenant agreement was advantageous to both parties because the covenant made both families more resilient and stronger than if they had stood alone (Copeland, 1989). For example, farmers may have joined forces with warriors so that all families under their covenant would be fed and protected at the same time. The Harris's who were farmers, entered entered into a covenant with the Burgs who were warriors and together they became the Harrisburg clan. Their differences were beneficial once they joined together to work as one unit.

This pattern of differences continues into marriage. Most of you have heard the old adage, "opposites attract." This is especially true in marriages, a covenant relationship. God in his infinite wisdom pairs spouses that are often as different as night and day. Unfortunately, most couples do not see their differences as assets. Typically, one spouse is trying to dominate and control the other so that the other spouse will conform to their attitudes and idiosyncrasies. The difficult part of this union is learning to work in harmony so that the family is strengthened and not divided. In order to strengthen the family with the diversity of gifts that are inherent in the husband and wife, the couple must not lean to their own understanding but seek the face of God for direction.

In the books of James and Ephesians the Lord has given instructions about how to maintain harmony in the marital relationship. First of all *submit yourself therefore to God (James 4:7). Husbands love your wives even as Christ also loved the church and gave himself for it (Ephesians 5:25). Wives submit yourselves unto your own husbands as unto the Lord, for the husband is the head of the wife even as Christ is the head of the church (Ephesians 5:22-23).* Then finally, *Submitting yourselves one to another in the fear of God (Ephesians 5:21).* All marriages will experience difficulties during the course of the marriage. However, getting through the storm successfully will take faith in God, praying, obeying, and submitting to his sovereign authority.

Are you in a covenant relationship either business or personal? What ceremony, vows, pledges, contracts were instituted to bind you into covenant with that other party?

_____

_____

_____

Has your covenant been broken? Does it need to be?

God's Moral Code

Our God is a sovereign God, an omnipotent God, a God that is worthy to be praised, obeyed, and respected. When Moses was on Mt. Sinai, the Most High God gave him a moral code for the Israelites that is still relevant today called the Ten Commandments. Unfortunately, the Ten Commandments have been taken out of public schools and all government buildings as to adhere to the constitutions amendment of separation of church and state. Although the Ten Commandments have all but disappeared out of public view do not let them disappear out of your heart, mind, and soul. Commit them to memory, teach them to your children, and grandchildren and live by God's moral code! *Therefore thou shalt keep the commandments of the Lord thy God, to walk in his ways, and to fear him (Deuteronomy 8:6).*

The Ten Commandments (Exodus 20:1-17)

- *Thou shall have no other gods before me*
- *Thou shall not make any graven images*
- *Thou shall not take the name of the Lord thy God in vain*
- *Thou shall not kill*
- *Thou shall not steal*
- *Honor thy father and thy mother that thy days be long upon the land which the Lord thy God giveth thee*
- *Thou shall not commit adultery*
- *Thou shall not bear false witness against thy neighbor*
- *Thou shall not covet thy neighbor's house, wife, or possessions*
- *Remember the Sabbath and keep it holy*

The Lord has given us instructions on how to live. He is telling us how to live for Him and how to live with others. During the time the commandments were written, individuals were stoned to death for breaking the laws. Aren't we glad that Jesus brought a new covenant that freed us from the law of sin and death. The commandments were written to convict us of unrighteousness so that we can strive to live a Holy life (Prince,2007).

In Matthew 22: 37-40, Jesus used two laws to summarize the commandments.

Thou shalt love the Lord thy God with all thy heart and with all thy soul and with all thy mind. This is the first and great commandment. And the second is like unto it, thou shalt love thy neighbor as thyself. On these two commandments hang all the law.

Let us hear the conclusion of the whole matter: fear God, and keep his commandments for this is the whole duty of man (Ecclesiastes 12:13).

God Does Not Always Call The Biggest And Brightest

God does not call you based on your earthly qualifications. Jesus chose ordinary men who were fishermen and tax collectors. He did not sit behind his desk and interview people with Ivy-League educations who lived in high rises or gated communities. He looks into your inner most being to determine if you have a heart for Him.

For ye see your calling brethren, that not many wise men, not many mighty, not many noble, are called. But God hath chosen the foolish things of the world to confound the wise and God hath chosen the weak things of the world to confound the things which are mighty (I Corinthians 1:26-27).

Have You Been Called?

God has a plan and a purpose for every living soul on the face of this planet. As part of the covenant relationship, the Lord will provide for you as you honor, submit, and obey Him. For decades, many of us in the body of Christ believed that if someone had a calling on their life it meant that they were destined to preach or go to the mission fields in third world countries. God has revealed to the body of Christ that not everyone is called to preach or to be a missionary. God has called people from all walks of life to follow Him and His way of doing things, not only in the church but in the marketplace.

Perhaps the Lord has called you to be a teacher, social worker, doctor, accountant, etc. There are no limitations with God. When you decide to do what God has called you to do, you will experience an inner peace and a strong desire to complete what God has planned. There will be many challenges and obstacles along the way but consult with the Lord and He will direct your path. As you say "yes" to your calling you will find that God has equipped you with the spiritual gifts you need to fulfill your calling.

How Were You Chosen?

Do you remember when the Lord called you? Although we were chosen before the foundation of the world, we usually don't understand that God is calling us until we are well into adulthood. It is my opinion that most of us have understood that the Lord was calling us before we reached the age of seventeen. It may have come in a dream or by prophesy, but somehow we knew and just dismissed it. Unfortunately many will say no, and others will delay saying yes to the Lord because of the belief that they will not be able to enjoy their life in the world's system. Others will say yes without completely submitting and making Jesus the Lord of their life. We have all heard about some preachers in our local communities or those who are internationally known who commit adultery, drink, use drugs, and are bound to being servants of men and not servants of God.

Many are called but few are chosen (Matthew 22:14). Ye have not chosen Me but I have chosen you, and ordained you. I have chosen you out of the world (John 15:16, 19). Ye are bought with a price be not servants of men (I Corinthians 7:23).

Benefits Of Your Calling

There are many benefits to your calling but the anointing you will receive has a price. Your training period to receive that anointing is determined by the Lord. Moses trained for eighty years before the Lord sent him to set His people free. Joseph was sold into slavery, accused of rape, and thrown into prison before he was promoted to his rightful position as second in command. If you are familiar with his story, he dreamed about it in early childhood.

Many of you are going through a training period and you feel like giving up. Stand strong and don't give up. The Book of Hebrews, chapter 11, will remind you of the faith that is required to step into your calling and receive the fullness of what God has predestined for you. The benefits will be great for those who are faithful and endure the purification process.

A man's gift maketh room for him and bringeth him before great men (Proverbs 18:16). Touch not mine anointed, and do my prophets no harm (I Chronicles 16:22). Walk worthy of God who hath called you unto his kingdom and glory (I Thessalonians 2:12).

Take a moment and meditate on what you have just read. These verses are just a reminder for some of you. Many of you have felt a stirring in your spirit for several years and ignored it. The uncertainty of what you were feeling and thinking paralyzed you into inaction. Perhaps these issues were not talked about with family and friends. Now that you understand that you have been called, take the next step. Sit with your eyes closed, turn off your phone, close out your e-mails and just be still. God is talking. Do not look at your watch, the Lord will tell you when He is through with you. Once you have surrendered yourself to the Most High God, write down what He has communicated to you.

_____

_____

What have you been called to do? Is it similar to what you are doing now?

_____

God reveals in parts. He may have told you that he wants you to start a Christian based homeless shelter and nothing else. That is the first step. In order to be successful with your assignment continue to pray and stay in the word of God. The Lord will tell you when and where to build and how to finance your project. Some of you may get all of the information at once and others will receive small bits of information several weeks to several months apart. Do not get discouraged, believe, pray, and have faith.

STEP NINE

DO NOT BE DECEIVED

Y ou may be well versed in keeping secrets and deceiving others but you cannot keep secrets from God. It is time to look at the different aspects of deception and it's effect on the body, soul, and spirit. Living a true and holy life is the only way to escape a life of deception and all of the negative consequences that ensue because of it. I strongly suggest that you give up that facade and follow Jesus.

> *Be not deceived, God is not mocked. For whatsoever a man soweth that shall he also reap (Galatians 6:7). For there is no man that doeth anything in secret (John 7:4).*

God's word was designed to teach us all truth as explained in the following verses. *Master, we know that thou art true, and teachest the way of God in truth (Matthew 22:16). That we should be to the praise of his glory who first trusted in Christ, In whom ye also trusted after that ye heard the word of truth, the gospel of your salvation in who also after that ye believed ye were sealed with that holy Spirit of promise (Ephesians 1:12-13).*

Living a Godly life, and a Christian life entails walking in the light of the Word, which is walking in truth. Truth is defined as honesty, fact, the real state of things, and actuality (Webster, 1998). The Bible is an instruction manual for living in truth under the kingdom of the one true living God. Living in truth will keep you out of bondage. The scripture says *and ye shall know the truth, and the truth shall make you free (John 8:32).*

Allow the following teaching to bring out the truth in you. This will be accomplished by breaking the word "truth" into its component parts.

(All definitions are taken from the Webster Dictionary, 1998 unless otherwise stated)

Truth
T   Teach, Testify
R   Repent, Renounce, Redemption
U   Unity
T   Treasure
H   Hope, Healing

In your lifetime, what truth was hidden from you? When it came to light how did it effect you or the people closest to you?

_____

_____

Teachers

Definition: one who guides the studies of, one who shows how, or one who imparts knowledge.

> *But the comforter which is the Holy Ghost whom the Father will send in my name he shall teach you all things and bring all things to your remembrance, whatsoever I have said unto you (John 22:26).*

All things are available to us on a supernatural level through the Holy Spirit. Although the Lord has given us the Holy Spirit as our supernatural teacher, He continues to provide guidance for us on this earthly plane through other teachers as part of the five-fold ministry gifts, *And he gave some apostles, and some prophets, and some evangelists and some pastors and some teachers. For the perfecting of the saints, for the work of the ministry (Ephesians 4:11-12).*

We are also taught by others who are not part of the five-fold ministry. God places people in our life to help guide and train. We live in the "world" and because of that many who guide and train in the workplace or in the education system are not Christians. You can learn higher mathematics from an agnostic. It is your job to represent Christ well and let His light shine through you.

What teachers have had a powerful influence in your life? If God had not put them in your life how would your life have been different?

_____

_____

Describe some things that were imparted or taught to you by your supernatural teacher the Holy Spirit?

_____

_____

Testify

Definition: to bear witness and make statements based on your personal experience or knowledge.

For I testify unto every man that heareth the words of the prophecy of this book (Revelations 22:18) For I have rejoiced greatly when the brethren came and testified of the truth that is in thee, even as thou walkest in truth (3 John 1:3). I might finish my course with joy and the ministry which I have received of the Lord Jesus, to testify the gospel of the grace of God (Acts 20:24).

Has anyone ever testified to you about Jesus? How did you receive the message?

_____

_____

> *And we have seen and do testify that the Father sent the Son to be the Savior of the world (I John 4:14).*

Have you ever told anyone about Jesus? Will you?

_____

_____

> *I Jesus have sent mine angel to testify unto you these things in the churches, I am the root and the offspring of David, and the bright and morning star (Revelation 22:17).*

Testify that Jesus is the Son of God, He is the way, the truth, and the life!

Repent/Renounce

Definitions: to repent means to turn away from sin and when you renounce something you give it up and refuse to follow or obey that person or doctrine.

If you have attended church for any length of time, it is quite likely that you have heard many sermons on repentance. Some of you wanted to buy the CD to give to a family member or friend. I have news for you, the message was for you as well. Allow the Holy Spirit to search the deepest recesses of your heart to bring up things that you have pushed below your level of awareness.

> *I tell you, Nay, but except ye repent, ye shall all likewise perish (Luke 13:3). But have renounced the hidden things of*

dishonesty, not walking in craftiness, nor handling the word of God deceitfully, but by manifestation of the truth commending ourselves to every man's conscience in the sight of God (2 Corinthians 4:2). From that time Jesus began to preach and to say, "Repent for the kingdom of heaven is at hand" (Matthew 4:17), repent and turn yourselves from your idols and turn away your faces from all your abominations (Ezekial 14:6).

Have you done or said anything lately that was out of the will of God? If so repent for it now, give it to Jesus, don't dwell on it, and do not be sin conscious.

Romans 8:1 says *There is therefore now no condemnation to them which are in Christ Jesus.* What is the Lord speaking to you now?

_____

_____

Redemption

Definition: to fulfill, to make good a promise, or to rescue by paying a price.

In Christ in whom we have redemption through his blood the forgiveness of sins, according to the riches of his grace (Ephesians 1:7). And grieve not the Holy Spirit of God whereby ye are sealed unto the day of redemption (Ephesians 4:30).

Now that you have a clearer understanding of what Jesus Christ has done for you, it is time to let go of that guilt and shame and live a life free of torment. You are redeemed. It is finished! It was finished at the cross on Calvary. Will you receive it today?

Unity

Definition: oneness, harmony, and working in one accord.

Behold, how good and how pleasant it is for brethren to dwell together in unity (Psalm 133:1). We all come in the unity of the faith, and of the knowledge of the Son of God unto a perfect man unto the measure of the stature of the fullness of Christ (Ephesians 4:13).

This principle of unity and working in one accord is evident when a natural disaster has plagued the land. Millions of dollars are raised, and thousands of people volunteer their time to help the victims. Think of the positive global impact unity would have on our society if we as humans would work together as one when there is no crisis.

Think about the last natural disaster that happened in your area or somewhere around the world. How did the world respond? How did you respond? Was there a stronger belief in God before, during, or after the disaster?

Treasure

Definition: something of great value, wealth that is stored.

For where your treasure is, there will your heart be also (Matthew 6:21). A good man out of the good treasure of the heart bringeth forth good things, and an evil man out of the evil treasure bringeth forth evil things (Matthew 12:35).

If we could peer into your hidden treasure what would we see?

_____

_____

The kingdom of heaven is like unto treasure hid in a field (Matthew 13:44).

The map to this treasure is located in Jesus Christ, it is hidden for and revealed to those who believe.

Hope

Definition: to desire with expectation, a promise for the future.

No matter the circumstances do not give up and let *the God of hope fill you with all joy and peace in believing that ye may abound in hope through the power of the Holy Ghost (Romans 15:13). To whom God would make known what is the riches of the glory of this mystery among the Gentiles, which is Christ in you, the hope of glory (Colossians 1:27).*

When you accept Jesus as your Lord and Savior stand on the promises of God and expect and hope to receive the riches of his glory.

What are you hoping for this day?

_____

_____

Healing

Definition: to make or become healthy, whole, to cure.

Do you need healing? Believe in the great physician, Jehovah Rapha. *And Jesus went about all Galilee teaching in their synagogues and preaching the gospel of the kingdom and healing all manner of sickness and all manner of disease among the people (Matthew 4:23). But unto you that fear my name shall the Sun of righteousness arise with healing in his wings (Malachi 4:2). But he was wounded for our transgressions, he was bruised for our iniquities, the chastisement of our peace was upon him, and with his stripes we are healed (Isaiah 53:5).*

The Spirit of the Lord is upon me because he hath anointed me to preach the gospel to the poor, he hath sent me to heal the broken hearted, to preach deliverance to the captives, and recovering of sight to the blind, to set at liberty them that are bruised, to preach the acceptable year of the Lord (Matthew 4:18-19).

Healing is part of God's "truth." Let your request be known to God. Healing is available for all of those who believe.

Do you need healing somewhere in your body? If so place your hand on that body part(s) pray the healing scriptures in Appendix D and then receive your healing.

Now that you have heard the word of truth, have you committed your life to the Lord and in what way?

Facade

When you are not walking in truth, then you are living a life that is full of deception, confusion, doubt, and the works of the flesh. What you are exhibiting is just a facade because it is not from God.

Facade is defined as an artificial or deceptive front (Hougton Mifflin, 1985). For illustrative purposes facade is broken down into several component parts.

F	Flesh, Fear
A	Anger
C	Confusion
A	Adultery and other sexual sins, Arrogance
D	Deception, Doubt
E	Enemy, Error

The following will enlighten you about the negative consequences of putting up a deceptive front.

Flesh

Definition: the soft tissue of the body, meat of animals, the body, or man's carnal nature.

Because we live in a body, the Bible has given us many instructions about how to combat the desires of the flesh and to walk in the spirit. In the seventh and eight chapters of Romans, the dichotomous nature of the flesh (which is our body and soul) is contrasted with the things of the Spirit. Determine the meaning of each verse according to the following descriptions. *(a) the body, (b) walking in the spirit, (c) a way of thinking, and (d) the human desires.* Some verses may have more than one meaning. Write your answer in the box provided by using the letters a, b, c, or d.

[ ] 1. *Watch and pray that ye enter not into temptation, the spirit indeed is willing but the flesh is weak (Matthew 26:41).*

[ ] 2. *For when we were in the flesh, the motions of sins which were by the law did work in our members to bring forth fruit unto death (Romans 7:5).*

[ ] 3. *For they that are after the flesh do mind the things of the flesh, but they that are after the Spirit the things of the Spirit (Romans 8:5).*

[ ] 4. *For to be carnally minded is death but to be spiritually minded is life and peace (Romans 8: 6).*

[ ] 5. *Because the carnal mind is enmity against God for it is not subject to the law of God, neither indeed can be (Romans 8: 7).*

[ ] 6. *So then they that are in the flesh cannot please God (Romans 8: 8).*

[ ] 7. *Therefore brethren we are debtors not to the flesh to live after the flesh (Romans 8: 12).*

[ ] 8. *For if ye live after the flesh, ye shall die but if ye through the Spirit do mortify the deeds of the body ye shall live (Romans 8: 13).*

[ ] 9. *I thank God through Jesus Christ our Lord. So then with the mind I myself serve the law of God but with the flesh the law of sin (Romans 7:25).*

[ ] 10. *For what the law could not do in that it was weak through the flesh, God sending his own Son in the likeness of sinful flesh, and for sin condemned sin in the flesh (Romans 8: 3).*

[ ] 11. *That the righteousness of the law might be fulfilled in us who walk not after the flesh but after the Spirit (Romans 8: 4).*

[ ] 12. *But ye are not in the flesh but in the Spirit if so be that the Spirit of God dwell in you. Now if any man have not the Spirit of Christ, he is none of his (Romans 8: 9).*

[ ] 13. *And if Christ be in you the body is dead because of sin but the Spirit is life because of righteousness (Romans 8: 10).*

[ ] 14. *But if the Spirit of him that raised up Jesus from the dead dwell in you, he that raised up Christ from the dead shall also quicken your mortal bodies by his Spirit that dwelleth in you (Romans 8: 11).*

[ ] 15. *There is therefore now no condemnation to them which are in Christ Jesus who walk not after the flesh but after the Spirit (Romans 8: 1).*

The carnal body seeks what is pleasurable and left unabated will quickly drown in excess as seen in drug addiction, gambling, over eating, and many other compulsive behaviors. However, as born again believers in Jesus Christ, we do not have to succumb to the desires of the flesh. Our victory is in the resurrection power of the Lord Jesus Christ.

For the law of the Spirit of life in Christ Jesus hath made me free from the law of sin and death (Romans 8:2).

Fear

Definition: to be afraid of, an awareness of danger, terror, or panic.

Fear is a very powerful emotion. It can be the underlying cause for many conditions such as anxiety, high blood pressure, headaches, nightmares, and a host of other problems (Bourne, 2000).

Fear hath torment, he that feareth is not made perfect in love (I John 4:18).

Fearfulness and trembling are come upon me and horror hath overwhelmed me (Proverbs 55:5).

My heart panted, fearfulness affrighted me, the night of my pleasure hath he turned into fear unto me (Isaiah 21:4).

When you are afraid what type of symptoms do you experience in your physical body?

_____

_____

When your fear cometh as desolation and your destruction cometh as a whirlwind when distress and anguish cometh upon you (Proverbs 1:27). Then shall they call upon me but I will not answer they shall seek me early but they shall not find me (Proverbs 1:28).

Were you ever in a situation that was so devastating that you were overcome by fear? Did you believe that God had turned his back on you?

_____

_____

What needs to be rectified in your life in order to drive out that spirit of fear?

_____

_____

Anger

Definition: fury, a strong feeling of displeasure, wrath, rage, or indignation.

Like lust, anger cannot be satisfied. The more you participate in it the more consuming it becomes.

> *For I was afraid of the anger and hot displeasure* (Deuteronomy 9:19). *Thus shall mine anger be accomplished and I will cause my fury to rest upon them (Ezekiel 5:13). There is no soundness in my flesh because of thine anger neither is there any rest in my bones because of my sin (Psalm 38:3). The dead bodies of men whom I have slain in my anger and my fury(Jeremiah 33:5).*

Have you lashed out at others in anger and at what cost? Explain the physical, verbal, and/or emotional pain your actions caused.

Confusion

Definition: to jumble, to mix up, something that is not clear.

Confusion brings anxiety, doubt, and an inability to make proper decisions. You struggle with what you want, what others expect, and what is right in God's eyes.

Read the following verses and describe how they apply to you in the space provided.

I am full of confusion therefore see thou mine affliction (Job 10:15). My confusion is continually before me and the shame of my face hath covered me (Psalm 44:15).

_____

_____

For where envying and strife is there is confusion and every evil work (James 3:12). We lie down in our shame and our confusion covereth us for we have sinned against the Lord our God, we and our fathers from our youth even unto this day and have not obeyed the voice of the Lord our God (Jeremiah 3:25).

_____

_____

Behold they are all vanity, their works are nothing, their molten images are wind and confusion (Isaiah 41:29).

_____

_____

Think about the times when you were most confused in your life. What was going on in your personal and professional life? How were you able to get out of turmoil? Who did you call?

> For God is not the author of confusion, but of peace.
> (I Corinthians 14:33)

Sexual Sin

The twentieth chapter of Leviticus is very clear about sexual sins, that is, what is unholy in the sight of Lord. In biblical times the penalty for violating most of these Levitical laws was death. In our society today, violating some of these laws, (sex with children) may lead to incarceration without the death penalty. The following verses describe incest, homosexuality, bestiality, lust, as well as adultery.

This will be the first time some of you have been exposed to these Bible verses. Talking about sex is uncomfortable for most people especially in Sunday sermons. After each section write down your thoughts and opinions about each sexual sin.

Adultery

Definition: when a married person is in a sexual relationship with someone else other than their spouse.

And the man that committeth adultery with another man's wife, even he that committeth adultery with his neighbor's wife, the adulterer and the adulteress shall surely be put to death (Leviticus 20:10).

But I say unto you, that whosoever looketh on a woman to lust after her hath committed adultery with her already in his heart (Matthew 5:28).

But as a wife that committeth adultery which taketh strangers instead of her husband (Ezekiel 16:32).

Ye adulterers and adulteresses know ye not that the friendship of the world is enmity with God (James 4:4).

Thoughts/Opinions

_____

_____

Incest

Definition: having sexual relationships with a family member.

The statistics are staggering about the rate of incest in the American population. The rate may be higher because of the shame and secrecy that accompanies this act. Many people will carry this secret to their graves. When incest is not talked about or dealt with properly it will continue from one generation to the next. If this is going on in your family or with someone you know use the prayers in Step 2 to break this curse. If the person being victimized is under eighteen notify the police and Child Protective Services in the state in which it is occurring and continue to pray for all involved.

And if a man lie with his daughter in law, both of them shall surely be put to death, they have wrought confusion, their blood shall be upon them (Leviticus 20:12).

And if a man shall take his sister, his father's daughter, or his mother's daughter and see her nakedness, and she see his nakedness, it is a wicked thing (Leviticus 20:17).

Thoughts/Opinions

_____

_____

Homosexuality

Definition: sexual attraction to a person of the same sex.

Many of you may have relatives that are living this life style. At the time of the writing of this book, all of the United States have already legalized same-sex marriages. It is not our job as Christians to hate them, but to love them and to pray for them. Remember this is a spiritual battle.

If a man also lie with mankind, as he lieth with a woman, both of them have committed an abomination. They shall surely be put to death, their blood shall be upon them (13).

And likewise also the men leaving the natural use of the woman burned in their lust one toward another, men with men working that which is unseemly, and receiving in themselves that recompense of their error which was meet (Romans 1:27).

Thoughts/Opinions

_____

_____

Bestiality

Definition: having sex with animals.

And if a man lie with a beast he shall surely be put to death and ye shall slay the beast (15).

Thoughts/Opinions

_____

_____

Lust

Definition: an intense sexual desire.

Thou has played the whore because thou was insatiable. How weak is thine heart saith the Lord God seeing thou doest all these things the work of an imperious whorish woman (Ezekiel 16:28, 30).

As stated before lust cannot be satisfied, it is a bottomless pit of desire. Contrary to popular belief, this too is a spiritual battle and can be prayed away. Music, movies, print media, and internet usage can stir the savage beast. Be careful what you allow to influence your mood and your way of thinking.

Thoughts/Opinions

_____

_____

The world's way of defining healthy sexuality does not always correspond with the Word of God. Give examples of how God's law is being violated in the world today concerning sexual relationships and sexual acts.

Arrogance

Definition: exaggerating one's own importance in an offensive or irritating manner.

If you continually act in an arrogant manner, then you are exalting yourself above the most High God. You can be confident without being arrogant. That is a revelation to some of you.

Talk no more exceeding proudly, let not arrogance come out of your mouth, for the Lord is a God of knowledge and by him actions are weighed (I Samuel 2:3).

Before destruction the heart of man is haughty and before honor is humility (Proverbs 18:12).

Deception

Definition: fraud, trickery, causing others to believe untruths.

In these last days it is important to stay in the word of God. There are many people claiming to be Christians but they have hidden agendas that are full of deception.

For many shall come in my name, saying I am Christ and shall deceive many (Matthew 24:5).

For there shall arise false Christs, and false prophets and shall show signs and wonders in so much that if it were possible they shall deceive the very elect (Matthew 24:24).

That we henceforth be no more children tossed to and fro and carried about with every wind of doctrine by the sleight of men and cunning craftiness, whereby they lie in wait to deceive (Ephesians 4:14). Just because it sounds good, looks good, smells good, and feels good, doesn't mean that it is good for *you!*

Let no man deceive you with vain words for because of these things cometh the wrath of God upon the children of disobedience (Ephesians 5:6).

We have all been deceived at some time in our lives. What incident hurt you the most and what was the final outcome?

_____

_____

Be not a witness against thy neighbor without cause, and deceive not with thy lips (Proverbs 24:28). Under what circumstances did you deceive others?

_____

_____

Error

Definition: deviating from the truth, mistakes.

Ye therefore beloved seeing ye know these things before beware lest ye also being led away with the error of the wicked fall from your own steadfastness (2 Peter 3:17).

Have you ever turned your back on the Lord? What led you away from the Lord and what brought you back?

_____

_____

Who can understand his errors? Cleanse thou me from secret faults (Psalm 19:12).

Are you living a secret life? What steps do you need to take to turn back to God?

_____

_____

Enemies

Definition: one that attacks or tries to harm another.

Deliver me from the hand of mine enemies and from them that persecute me (Psalm 31:15). So let all thine enemies perish (Judges 5:31). And you that were sometime alienated and enemies in your mind by wicked works, yet now hath he reconciled (Colossians 1:27).

And stay ye not, but pursue after your enemies (Joshua 10:19). Mine enemies speak evil of me (Psalm 41:5). Mine enemies reproach me while they say daily unto me, Where is thy God? (Psalm 42:10).

Have you ever been in a situation where you were surrounded by people who mocked your belief in God? Did it feel as if the Lord had abandoned you for that moment? How did you get out of the situation?

_____

_____

The Bible says to pray for those who despitefully use you. Pursue your enemies with prayer. You ask, what do I pray? Start with Ephesians 3:17-19. When you are comfortable enough to venture out on your own use any scriptures that are relevant to your situation

As you can see, facade leads to destruction of self, destruction of others, chaos, and confusion. Trusting in the Lord leads to **The Way, The Truth, and The Life.** Which road will you choose, **Truth or Facade?** The choice is yours.

STEP TEN

RESIST

The addiction community posits that relapse is part of recovery. There are many trials and tribulations that will afflict us in this lifetime. Don't get upset if you go back to your old ways of behaving or thinking the minute you become overwhelmed. After all, you have practiced it for quite some time, maybe even years. The important thing is not to stay there by justifying your negative behavior and attitudes. By now you have learned new coping skills and you have a heavenly support system.

And have no fellowship with the unfruitful works of darkness (Ephesians 5:11). Wherein times past ye walked according to the course of this world, according to the prince of the power of the air, the spirit that now worketh in the children of disobedience (Ephesians 2:2). Submit yourselves therefore to God. Resist the devil, and he will flee from you (James 4:7).

The following section contains situations and thought patterns characterized by many individuals who are struggling with strongholds. Often times, people lie to themselves when they aren't willing to change or do not know how to change. It is easy to get caught in a web of self-deception. What is important is to face the truth and let God show you what He can do for you. Many of you need supernatural intervention to be set free because until now nothing else has worked for you on a consistent basis.

At the beginning of each category is a Bible verse that describes the problem, followed by examples of the problem. The solution to break your negative way of thinking and behaving is also a Bible verse(s). These verses are taken from the book of Proverbs.

Problems and Solutions

Problem: Hope deferred maketh the heart sick, and a broken spirit drieth the bones (Proverbs 13:12, 17:22).

- *I dropped out of college to get married. I want to finish my degree but I have three small children.*
- *I have been really depressed because of the divorce and all the debt that I was left with.*
- *I want to be debt free. Now, I am almost 50 and still paying bills.*

Solution: The blessing of the Lord, it maketh rich and addeth no sorrow with it. A merry heart doeth good like a medicine and when the desire cometh it is a tree of life. For wisdom is better than rubies, and all things desired are not to be compared to it (Proverbs 10:22, 17:22, 13:12, 8:11).

Problem: Every one that is proud in heart is an abomination to the Lord (Proverbs 16:5).

- *Other people tell me I am arrogant, self-centered, and lack compassion. It's a tough world and I have to look out for myself.*
- *I am always the life of the party and can get any man I want.*
- *I am climbing the corporate ladder and I am good at what I do. Sometimes I do things that are unethical, but never illegal, in order to get ahead.*

Solution: By mercy and truth iniquity is purged, and by the fear of the Lord men depart from evil (Proverbs 16:6).

Problem: There is a generation that are pure in their own eyes, and yet is not washed from their filthiness (Proverbs 30:12).

- *I know its illegal and I am not forcing anyone to do anything against their will. I will stop when there is no longer a demand for my services.*
- *My husband doesn't hit me all the time and besides I have never been hospitalized for my injuries. I have a plan, he is going to get his . . .*
- *My father was like this and nothing happened to him. It runs in our family. Don't worry.*

Solution: Envy thou not the oppressor, and choose none of his ways. Discretion shall preserve thee, understanding shall keep thee. Forget not my law, but let thine heart keep my commandments. For length of days and long life and peace shall they add to thee (Proverbs 3:31, 2:11, 3:1-2).

Problem: Fools despise wisdom and instruction. He that hath no rule over his own spirit is like a city that is broken down and without walls (Proverbs 1:7, 25:28).

- *There is nothing wrong with me, I'm not crazy. I don't need counseling or medication. I can talk to my friends and have a drink.*
- *I have to use, I have had a hard life and things never work out for me.*
- *I am not like other people, I can stop anytime.*

Solution: Avoid it, pass not by it, turn from it, and pass away. A wise man will hear, and will increase learning, and a man of understanding shall attain unto wise counsel (Proverbs 4:15, 1:5).

---

12 Steps To Overcoming Tragic Life Events

Problem: In the greatness of his folly he shall go astray (Proverbs 5:23)

- *I make enough money to have a wife and two girlfriends. As long as they don't know about each other everything is fine.*
- *There is nothing wrong with having cyber sex and besides I have never met those people in person. My spouse travels all of the time, leaving me alone and I don't see any harm in it.*
- *We belong to a swinger's club to keep the excitement going in our marriage. We decided that if we consent to have sex with others while we are together that it can't be considered adultery.*

Solution: Trust in the Lord with all thine heart, and lean not unto thine own understanding. In all thy ways acknowledge him, and he shall direct thy paths (Proverbs 3:5-6).

Problem: He also that is slothful in his work is brother to him that is a great waster and wealth gotten by vanity shall be diminished (Proverbs 18:9, 13:11).

- *I do just enough at work so that I do not lose my job. Besides they don't me pay enough anyway.*
- *I rent an office/apartment with all bills paid. When I am not there, I leave the lights on and the a/c on full blast. I want to get my money's worth.*
- *I am in the entertainment/sports industry. I make more in a day than most people can make in a year because of my talent. God didn't do this, I did this.*
- *Once my kids turn eighteen they are on their own. After all, no one helped me when I was their age.*

112

Solution: The fear of the Lord is to hate evil, pride, and arrogancy. He that gathereth by labor shall increase. Through wisdom is an house builded and by understanding it is established. A good man leaveth an inheritance to his children (Proverbs 8:13, 13:11, 24:3, 13:22).

Snap Out Of It

Maladaptive behaviors and thoughts are formed through repetition. In order to combat these habits put on a wrist band of your choosing. Snap it and say a Bible verse every time you find yourself falling back into the negative behaviors and thought patterns. This is another weapon in your arsenal to defeat the enemy. *Now the hand of the Lord was upon me (Ezekiel 33:22) and God by his hand would deliver them (Acts 7:25).*

What negative thoughts or habits are you trying to break?

_____

_____

What Bible verses are you going to speak to break them?

_____

_____

STEP ELEVEN

BE THANKFUL AND PRAISE THE LORD

It is quite likely that you have a closer relationship with the Lord than when you first started this book. Some of you have already been healed, delivered and set free by the glory of God. For others it will take longer but don't be dismayed, help is on the way. Continue to pray and believe.

This is the day the Lord hath made, we will rejoice and be glad in it (Psalm 118:24).

Just as you did in Step One, peruse the following list of the names of God. Find the names that describe your relationship with the Lord and explain why in the space provided at the end of this section.

Other Names for Jesus and Bible Verses

Emmanuel God With Us (Matthew 1:23) Behold a virgin shall be with child and shall bring forth a son. And they shall call His name Emmanuel which being interpreted is God with us.

The Son of The Living God (Matthew 16:16) And Simon Peter answered and said, thou art the Christ, the Son of the living God.

The Dayspring From On High (Luke 1:78) Through the tender mercy of our God, whereby the dayspring from on high hath visited us.

The Word (John 1:1) In the beginning was the Word and the Word was with God and the Word was God.

The Lamb Of God (John 1:29) The next day John seeth Jesus coming unto him and saith, behold the Lamb of God which taketh away the sin of the world.

The Light Of The World (John 8:12) Then spake Jesus again unto them saying, I am the light of the world, he that followeth me shall not walk in darkness but shall have the light of life.

The Resurrection And The Life (John 11:25-26) Jesus said unto her I am the resurrection and the life, he that believeth in me, though he were dead, yet shall he live.

The Way, The Truth, And The Life (John 14:6) Jesus saith unto him, I am the way, the truth, and the life, no man cometh unto the Father but by me.

The Holy One (Acts 3:14) But ye denied the Holy One and just and desired a murderer to be granted unto you.

The Rock (I Corinthians 10:4) And did all drink the same spiritual drink, for they drank of that spiritual Rock that followed them and that Rock was Christ.

A Merciful and Faithful High Priest (Hebrews 2:17) Wherefore in all things it behooved him to be made like unto his brethren that he might be a merciful and faithful high priest in things pertaining to God, to make reconciliation for the sins of the people.

The Author And Finisher Of Our Faith (Hebrews 12:2) Looking unto Jesus the author and finisher of our faith, who for the joy that was set before him endured the cross, despising the shame, and is set down at the right hand of the throne of God.

The Savior (Philippians 3:20) For our conversation is in heaven, from whence also we look for the Savior, the Lord Jesus Christ.

The Propitiation For Our Sins (I John 2:2) And he is the propitiation for our sins, and not for ours only, but also for the sins of us the whole world.

The Firstborn From The Dead (Revelation 1:5) And from Jesus Christ who is the faithful witness and the first begotten of the dead and the prince of the kings of the earth unto him that loved us, and washed us from our sins in his own blood.

The Alpha and the Omega (Revelation 1:8) I am Alpha and Omega, the beginning and the ending saith the Lord, which is and which was, and which is to come, the Almighty.

The Lion of the Tribe of Judah (Revelation 5:5) And of the elders saith unto me, weep not, behold the Lion of the tribe of Judah, the root of David hath prevailed to open the book and to loose the seven seals thereof.

Bright and Morning Star (Revelation 22:16) I Jesus have sent mine angel to testify unto you these things in the churches. I am the root and the offspring of David and the bright and morning star.

The Redeemer (Job 19:25) For I know that my redeemer liveth and that he shall stand at the latter day upon the earth.

The Friend Who Sticks Closer Than A Brother (Proverbs 18:24) A man that hath friends must show himself friendly and there is a friend that sticketh closer than a brother.

The Prince of Peace, Wonderful Counselor (Isaiah 9:6) For unto us a child is born, unto us a son is given and the government shall be upon his shoulder and his name shall be called Wonderful Counselor, The Mighty God, The everlasting Father, The Prince of Peace.

Now that you have identified what the Lord means to you it is time to get a deeper understanding and incorporate your appreciation of the Lord into every area of your life. At the end of each section write down the names of God that you believe are reflected in the verses that are found in Steps One and Eleven. You may also use these verses as prayers. Personalize the prayers by changing the pronouns to fit your situation and include the different names of God for power-packed prayers.

Thank The Lord For Who He Is

Give thanks unto the Lord, call upon his name, make known his deeds among the people (I Chronicles 16:8).

Example: I give thanks unto the Lord, my savior and my redeemer. I call upon His name and make known his deeds among the people.

For His Mercy

Oh give thanks unto the Lord for he is good, for his mercy endureth forever (I Chronicles 16:34).

For His Wisdom And Knowledge

Blessed be the name of God for ever and ever, for wisdom and might are his. He changeth the times and the seasons, he removeth kings, and setteth up kings. He giveth wisdom unto the wise and knowledge to them that know understanding. He revealeth the deep and secret things, he knoweth what is in the darkness, and the light dwelleth with him (Daniel 2:21-22). Thanks be unto to God, which always causeth us to triumph in Christ (2 Corinthians 3:14).

Thank The Lord For Who You Are And What He Has Done For You

Bless the Lord, O my soul and all that is within me (Psalm 103:1). I thank thee and praise thee O thou God of my fathers, who hast given me wisdom and might (Daniel 1:23).

For His Guidance

The Lord is my shepherd I shall not want. He maketh me to lie down in green pastures, he leadeth me beside the still waters. He restoreth my soul He leadeth me in the paths of righteousness for his name's sake.

For His Protection

Yea, though I walk through the valley of the shadow of death, I will fear no evil. For thou art with me, thy rod and thy staff they comfort me. Thou preparest a table before me in the presence of mine enemies. Thou anointest my head with oil, my cup runneth over. Surely goodness and mercy shall follow me all the days of my life and I will dwell in the house of the Lord for ever (Psalm 23).

Thank The Lord For Others

Through Prayer

We give thanks to God and the Father of our Lord Jesus Christ, praying always for you (Colossians 1:3).

Through Faith And Love

We are bound to thank God always for you brethren that your faith groweth exceedingly and the charity of everyone of you all toward each other aboundeth. So that we ourselves glory in you in the churches of God for your patience and faith in all your persecutions and tribulations that ye endure (2 Thessalonians 1:3-4).

We Are Worthy

Which is a manifest token of the righteous judgment of God, that ye may be counted worthy of the kingdom of God for which ye also suffer (2 Thessalonians 1:5).

Thank The Lord For Your Food And Provisions

In The Wilderness

Stop murmuring and complaining about your present circumstances because it won't last. Look to the Most High for guidance so that you do not die in the wilderness. God will bring you through. Suffering is part of the human condition, no one escapes. The important thing is not to give up and turn away from God when the going gets tough.

And thou shalt remember all the way which the Lord thy God led thee these forty years in the wilderness to humble thee, to prove thee, to know what was in thine heart. Whether thou wouldest keep his commandments or no. And he humbled thee to hunger, and fed thee with manna which thou knewest not, neither did thy fathers know that he might make thee know that man doth not live by bread alone, but by every word that proceedeth out of the mouth of the Lord doth man live (Deuteronomy 8: 1-3).

For Your Inheritance In The Promise Land

It is never too late to enter into the Kingdom of God through the promises of God. Your earthly inheritance awaits. At this point, you should know who you are and who God predestined you to be. Others of you may have become very successful without acknowledging the fact that the Lord allowed you to obtain your wealth. Now that you know better, refocus and use your God-given talents under the direction of our loving, heavenly Father.

For the Lord thy God bringeth thee into a good land . . . a land wherein thou shalt eat bread without scareness, thou shalt not lack any thing in it. Thou say in thine heart my power and the might of mine hand hath gotten me this wealth. But that shall remember the Lord thy God, for it is he that giveth thee power to get wealth that he may establish his covenant which he swear unto thy fathers as it is this day (Deuteronomy 8: 7,9,17,18).

Give God The Glory

Have you noticed that many entertainers and athletes thank God when they win or accept an award. What you have contributed to your family, friends, or workplace may never be recognized with pomp and ceremony. The omniscient God is aware of everything you do, and He thanks you for serving Him. Now thank Him for everything He does.

Thou shalt bless the Lord thy God for the good land which he hath given thee (Deuteronomy 8:10). Stand every morning to thank and praise the Lord (I Chronicles 23:30). I will call upon the Lord who is worthy to be praised. The Lord is my rock and my fortress, my deliverer, my God, my strength, in whom I will trust, my buckler, and the horn of my salvation and my high tower (Psalm 18:3, 2).

In Prayer, Praise, And Worship Give Thanks

Some people only praise and worship the Lord when they attend church, what about you? The scriptures says to praise and pray continuously with your voice, with your instruments, and with your dance. Do not be selfish with your prayers. Pray for all people and all nations.

They lifted up their voice with the trumpets and cymbals and instruments of music and praised the Lord (2 Chronicles 5:13). I will praise thee, O Lord among the people, I will sing unto thee among the people. I will sing unto thee among the nations (Psalm 57:9) I exhort therefore, that first of all, supplications, prayers, intercessions, and giving of thanks be made for all men (I Timothy 2:1). Let us offer the sacrifice of praise to God continually that is the fruit of our lips giving thanks to his name (Hebrews 13:15).

Minister And Prophesy With Thanks

This message is for the five-fold ministry gifts of the apostles, prophets, evangelists, pastors and teachers. Do you always bring a message of doom and gloom? Do you continuously scold the congregation? The Lord wants you to balance the equation with thanks and praise and to minister with love.

I thank Christ Jesus our Lord who hath enabled me, for he counted me faithful putting me into the ministry (I Timothy 1:12). Jeduthan who prophesied with a harp to give thanks and to praise the Lord (I Chronicles 25:3). And Hezekiah appointed the courses of the priests and the Levites after their courses, every man according to his service, the priests and Levites for burnt offerings and for peace offerings. To minister and to give thanks and to praise in the gates of the tents of the Lord (2 Chronicles 31:2).

Give Thanks To The Lord With Sacrifices, Offering & Tithes

Now ye have consecrated yourselves unto the Lord, come near and bring sacrifices and thank offerings into the house of the Lord (2 Chronicles 29:31). Bring the sacrifice of praise unto the Lord (Psalm 33:11). Bring you all the tithes into the storehouse, that there may be meat in mine house saith the Lord of hosts (Malachi 3:10).

> *In everything give thanks. For this is the will of God in Christ Jesus concerning you.*
>
> *(I Thessalonians 5:18)*

STEP TWELVE

SEEK THE LORD AND DO NOT LOOK BACK

As part of Step Twelve you will need to go back and read your life story. This will be the last time in this twelve step process that you will be allowed to focus on your past hurt and pain. When you are done answer the following questions.

How have you reconciled what has happened to you in your lifetime?

_____

_____

Who does God say that you are?

_____

_____

If you were unable to give positive answers to the questions, STOP, and go back to the step(s) where you are stuck. Proceed to Step 12 when you are free from the bondage and strongholds of the past. Pray and listen. Let God direct you to your healing. Which step(s) will you need to repeat before you work Step 12?

_____

_____

Who do you need to forgive?

_____

_____

Seek ye first the Kingdom of God, and his righteousness and all these things shall be added unto you (Matthew 6:33).

This is the last step on your journey to recovery from the past. Do not look back, nor to the left nor to the right. God is going to help you fulfill your destiny. Now is the time to make God the Lord of your life. Consult the great I AM before you do anything. All major decisions in your life are not to be made without first consulting the Lord. He is your father, your spouse, the CEO of your business. Incorporate Him into every area of your life and watch things change for the better.

Look not back for fear was round about saith the Lord (Jeremiah 46:5). Escape for thy life, look not behind thee (Genesis 19:17). According to his promise look for a new heaven and a new earth wherein dwelleth righteousness (2 Peter 3:13).

Many of you have spent most of your life living in fear because of the tragic life events you have suffered. The Lord is saying that if you want a new life, do not look back. Stay grounded in the present and prepare for the future.

Pitfalls

In this section I have included three pitfalls to be aware of that will hinder your deliverance and your relationship with the Lord if you do not make the necessary changes.

Idolatry

Idolatry is defined as excessive devotion or the worship of a physical object as god (Webster, 1998). Some of you are saying that you would never worship anything besides the one true living God. However, if you are devoting more time and energy to another person, to a job, or to a business than you spend with God, or if you do not start your day with prayer, or consult with God before making major decisions then you are in idolatry. Do not get angry about this statement. It was designed to get your attention. If you have been guilty of practicing idolatry, repent before the Lord and rectify the situation. When you don't seek God first and are over focused on other matters, you run the risk of making bad decisions and being out of the will of God. All the clutter in your head will muffle the voice of God and the direction He has for your life.

What changes are you going to make in your life in order to put God first?

_____

_____

False Gods

There are many dark spirits that call themselves god. These false gods have permeated our society with magic tricks, false prophesies, counterfeit miracles. You may have attended séances, had your palm read, and seen furniture levitate. Do not be impressed. After all Satan is the god of this world and he has supernatural power.

What is your zodiac sign? Never answer that question again as a born again believer of Jesus Christ. Stop reading your daily horoscope. No longer designate or identify yourself by that zodiac sign and discard those symbols.

New Age philosophy is now running rampant in many Christian churches. Some churches are so seeker-sensitive and focused on building large congregations that they have failed to teach, preach, or exalt the one true living God. The doctrine of the one world religion and mixing your faith with other religions is growing rapidly. All of this is used to cause doubt and deception in the body of Christ and to render it powerless.

An evil and adulterous generation seeketh after a sign (Matthew 12:39). Regard not them that have familiar spirits, neither seek after wizards to be defiled by them. I am the Lord your God (Leviticus 19:31). Beware of false prophets which come to you in sheep's clothing, but inwardly they are ravening wolves. Ye shall know them by their fruits (Matthew 7:15-16).

What false prophets were part of your life and how did they influence you?

_____

_____

Throw out their books, CDs, DVDs, and delete their digital communications as soon as possible!

What is your position or rank in God's army? Get quiet before the Lord and write down His response. Receive it by faith.

_____

_____

If you are ready to live for God then adhere to the advice in the following verse of scripture. *If my people which are called by my name, shall humble themselves and pray and seek my face and turn from their wicked ways, then will I hear from heaven and will forgive their sin and heal their land (2 Chronicles 7:14).*

Other Worldly Things

Many of you belong to social and fraternal organizations that involved initiations and making vows as part of the indoctrination process. Did you make a vow to a Greek God or a Luciferian doctrine? This is an example of other worldly things. Before you get offended, look up the history of your organization. Research the founding members to determine who you are really aligned with and have made vows to. The enemy hides and seduces God's people through good works. If you have not been able to receive a promotion in your professional life, and are stunted in your personal and spiritual growth, then this may be your road block.

In order to go to a higher spiritual level in the kingdom of God it is necessary to renounce those vows and pledges. Say this out loud:

In the name of Jesus Christ of Nazareth, I renounce all pledges, vows, and oaths I took as a member of (organization). I sever all soul ties between me and all members of (organization). I am cleansed by the blood of the lamb and the Lord has loosed me from my bonds. O Lord truly I am thy servant and I will pay my vows to you and to you only. In Jesus' name I pray, Amen.

List the ways you are going to incorporate Step 12 into your life.

_____

_____

Conclusion

*C*ongratulations! You have completed Part I. The Way, The Truth, and The Life is no longer a mystery to you. Now you have your heavenly instruction manual. The Lord has done a good work in you.

These are the twelve steps, to staying free.
12 Steps TOTLE (To Overcoming Tragic Life Events)

Step One   Say the Name
Step Two   Confess that Jesus is the Son of God
Step Three   Repent
Step Four   Forgive
Step Five   Pray
Collectively, Steps 1-5 lead to Step 6.
Step Six   Deliverance from strongholds

If you say the name of Jesus, confess that He is the Son of God, repent for your sins, forgive those who have hurt you, pray without ceasing, then the Lord, God almighty will deliver you from your afflictions.

He shall deliver thee in six troubles, yea in seven there shall no evil touch thee (Job 5:19).

Steps 7-12 show the battle we are in on a daily basis, the battle between good and evil. Follow these steps to defeat the forces of evil unto victory.

Evil	Good
Step Seven—Rebuke Satan	Step Eight—Submit To God
Step Nine—Don't let Satan deceive you	Step Eleven—Thank the Lord
Step Ten—Resist Satan	Step Twelve—Seek the Lord

By completing 12 Steps To Overcoming Tragic Life Events, like Job, you have told your story. You have overcome through repentance, forgiveness, and by the Word of the most High God. While you were lost in the quagmire of despair, God sent someone to speak life into your soul, and in the midst of it, God himself showed up.

Now that you have been delivered and set free when will you share these steps with others so that they can experience the goodness of God?

THE 12 STEP MANDATE

Be ye not ashamed of the Gospel of Christ (Romans 1:16a) and go into all the world and preach the gospel to every creature (Mark 16:15). Repentance and remission of sins should also be preached in His name to all nations (Luke 24:47), confirming the Word with signs following (Mark 16:20). Because it is the power of God unto salvation to every one that believeth (Romans 1:16). Whosoever findeth Christ, findeth life (Proverbs 8:35), and he that believeth not shall be damned (Mark 16:16b). Be not weary in well doing (Galatians 6:9) because you can do all things through Christ who strengthens you (Phillippians 4:13).

It is time for you to let go of your past and delve deeper into the word of God. Part II is a study guide for twelve books of the Bible that correspond to the twelve steps of this book and is entitled *"Seek Ye First The Kingdom of God."* Let's get started!

About The Author

D r. Julia Floyd Jones began her career in the mental health field and has worked in psychiatric hospitals, treatment centers, community based agencies, and private practice. She specialized in the treatment of posttraumatic stress disorder, sexual abuse, sexual addiction, substance abuse, depression, and eating disorders.

Julia has earned a B.A. in psychology from the University of Texas at Dallas, and a M.A. and Ph.D. in counseling psychology from Texas Woman's University. She is a marketplace minister, a prophetic painter, evangelist, counselor, and teacher.

She is founder and president of Global Affairs Ministries and Artist and Scribe, LLC that serves the local community and the world with signs and wonders following.

She has also written *Seek Ye First The Kingdom of God* which is the second book in this series. It is available directly form the publisher or from all online booksellers. To contact Dr. Julia Floyd Jones visit www.artistandscribe.com.

APPENDIX A

$\mathcal{P}$RAYERS

The Proverbial Prayer is taken from the book of Proverbs, and is for this 12 Step Program. Read it out loud before you begin your day or as you end your day. Use it as you will, and let the Spirit of the Most High God infuse you with his power.

PROVERBIAL PRAYER

God is a shield unto them that put their trust in Him (30:5). Therefore I will trust in the Lord with all my heart and lean not unto my own understanding because the fear of the Lord is the beginning of wisdom (9:10), and understanding is a wellspring of life (16:22).

I will keep God's commandments for length of days and long life, and peace shall they add to me (3:1-2). I will keep my heart with all diligence for out of it are the issues of life (4:23). Every word of God is pure (30:5). Death and life are in the power of the tongue (18:21).

Discretion shall preserve me and understanding shall keep me (2:11) and by mercy and truth, iniquity is purged from me (16:6). In all my ways I will acknowledge God and He shall direct my path (3:5-6).

MATTHEW 6:9-13
The Lord's Prayer

(9) Our Father which are in heaven, hallowed be thy name. (10) Thy Kingdom come, thy will be done in earth as it is in heaven. (11) Give us this day our daily bread. (12) And forgive us our debts as we forgive our debtors. (13) And lead us not into temptation, but deliver us from evil, for thine is the kingdom, and the power, and the glory, forever, Amen.

PSALM 23
The Lord Is My Shepherd

(1) The Lord is my shepherd, I shall not want. (2) He maketh me to lie down in green pastures, he leadeth me beside the still waters, (3) He restoreth my soul, he leadeth me in the paths of righteousness for his name's sake. (4) Yea, though I walk through the valley of the shadow of death, I will fear no evil, for thou art with me, thy rod and thy staff they comfort me. (5) Thou prepares a table before me in the presence of mine enemies, thou anointest my head with oil, my cup runneth over. (6) Surely goodness and mercy shall follow me all the days of my life, and I will dwell in the house of the Lord forever.

PSALM 100
A Psalm Of Praise

(1) Make a joyful noise unto the Lord all ye lands. (2) Serve the Lord with gladness, come before his presence with singing. (3) Know ye that the Lord he is God, it is he that hath made us and not we ourselves, we are his people and the sheep of his pasture. (4) Enter into his gates with thanksgiving, and into his courts with praise, be thankful unto him and bless his name.

(5) For the Lord is good, his mercy is everlasting, and his truth endureth to all generations.

PSALM 103:1-5
A Psalm of Blessings

Bless the Lord, O my soul and all that is within me, bless his holy name. (2) Bless the Lord, O my soul and forget not all his benefits, (3) Who forgiveth all thine iniquities, who healeth all thy diseases. (4) Who redeemeth thy life from destruction, who crowneth thee with loving-kindness and tender mercies. (5) Who satisfieth thy mouth with good things so that thy youth is renewed like the eagle's.

EPHESIANS 6:10-19
The Whole Armor Of God

Finally my brethren be strong in the Lord and in the power of his might. (11) Put on the whole armor of God that ye may be able to stand against the wiles of the devil. (12) For we wrestle not against flesh and blood, but against principalities, against powers, against the rulers of the darkness of this world, against spiritual wickedness in high places. (13) Wherefore take unto you to you the whole armor of God, that ye may be able to withstand in the evil day, and having done all to stand. (14) Stand therefore having your loins girt about with truth, and having on the breastplate of righteousness, (15) and your feet shod with the preparation of the gospel of peace. (16) Above all taking the shield of faith, wherewith ye shall be able to quench all the fiery darts of the wicked. (17) and take the helmet of salvation, and the sword of the spirit which is the word of God. (18) Praying always with all prayer and supplication in the Spirit and watching thereunto with all perseverance and supplication for all saints. (19) And for me, that utterance may be given unto me that I may open my mouth boldly to make known the mystery of the gospel.

𝓗EALING SCRIPTURES

Exodus 15:26

(26) And said, If thou wilt diligently hearken to the voice of the LORD thy God, and wilt do that which is right in his sight, and wilt give ear to his commandments, and keep all his statutes, I will put none of these diseases upon thee, which I have brought upon the Egyptians: for I am the LORD that healeth thee.

Exodus 23:25-26

(25) And ye shall serve the LORD your God, and he shall bless thy bread, and thy water; and I will take sickness away from the midst of thee. (26) There shall nothing cast their young, nor be barren, in thy land: the number of thy days I will fulfill.

Deuteronomy 7:15

(15) And the LORD will take away from thee all sickness, and will put none of the evil diseases of Egypt, which thou knowest, upon thee; but will lay them upon all them that hate thee.

Psalm 91:9-10

(9) Because thou hast made the LORD, which is my refuge, even the most High, thy habitation; (10) There shall no evil befall thee, neither shall any plague come nigh thy dwelling.

Psalm 103:1-5

(1) Bless the LORD, O my soul: and all that is within me, bless his holy name. (2) Bless the LORD, O my soul, and forget not all

his benefits: (3) Who forgiveth all thine iniquities; who healeth all thy diseases; (4) Who redeemeth thy life from destruction; who crowneth thee with lovingkindness and tender mercies; (5) Who satisfieth thy mouth with good things; so that thy youth is renewed like the eagle's.

Psalm 107:19-20

(19) Then they cry unto the LORD in their trouble, and he saveth them out of their distresses. (20) He sent his word, and healed them, and delivered them from their destructions.

Proverbs 4:20-23

(20) My son, attend to my words; incline thine ear unto my sayings. (21) Let them not depart from thine eyes; keep them in the midst of thine heart. (22) For they are life unto those that find them, and health to all their flesh. (23) Keep thy heart with all diligence; for out of it are the issues of life.

Isaiah 41:10

"Fear thou not; for I am with thee: be not dismayed; for I am thy God: I will strengthen thee; yea, I will help thee; yea, I will uphold thee with the right hand of my righteousness."

Isaiah 53:4-5

(4) Surely he hath borne our griefs, and carried our sorrows: yet we did esteem him stricken, smitten of God, and afflicted. (5) But he was wounded for our transgressions, he was bruised for our iniquities: the chastisement of our peace was upon him; and with his stripes we are healed.

Isaiah 55:9-11

(9) For as the heavens are higher than the earth, so are my ways higher than your ways, and my thoughts than your thoughts.

(10) For as the rain cometh down, and the snow from heaven, and returneth not thither, but watereth the earth, and maketh it bring forth and bud, that it may give seed to the sower, and bread to the eater: (11) So shall my word be that goeth forth out of my mouth: it shall not return unto me void, but it shall accomplish that which I please, and it shall prosper in the thing whereto I sent it.

Isaiah 58:6-11

(6) Is not this the fast that I have chosen? To loose the bands of wickedness, to undo the heavy burdens, and to let the oppressed go free, and that ye break every yoke? (7) Is it not to deal thy bread to the hungry, and that thou bring the poor that are cast out to thy house? When thou seest the naked, that thou cover him; and that thou hide not thyself from thine own flesh? (8) Then shall thy light break forth as the morning, and thine health shall spring forth speedily: and thy righteousness shall go before thee; the glory of the LORD shall be thy rearward. (9) Then shalt thou call, and the LORD shall answer; thou shalt cry, and he shall say, Here I am. If thou take away from the midst of thee the yoke, the putting forth of the finger, and speaking vanity; (10) And if thou draw out thy soul to the hungry, and satisfy the afflicted soul; then shall thy light rise in obscurity, and thy darkness be as the noonday: (11) And the LORD shall guide thee continually, and satisfy thy soul in drought, and make fat thy bones: and thou shalt be like a watered garden, and like a spring of water, whose waters fail not.

Jeremiah 30:17

(17) For I will restore health unto thee, and I will heal thee of thy wounds, saith the LORD; because they called thee an Outcast, saying, This is Zion, whom no man seeketh after.

Malachi 4:2-3

(2) But unto you that fear my name shall the Sun of righteousness arise with healing in his wings; and ye shall go forth, and grow up as calves of the stall.(3) And ye shall tread down the wicked; for they shall be ashes under the soles of your feet in the day that I shall do this, saith the LORD of hosts.

Matthew 7:7-11

(7) Ask, and it shall be given you; seek, and ye shall find; knock, and it shall be opened unto you: (8) For every one that asketh receiveth; and he that seeketh findeth; and to him that knocketh it shall be opened. (9) Or what man is there of you, whom if his son ask bread, will he give him a stone? (10) Or if he ask a fish, will he give him a serpent? (11) If ye then, being evil, know how to give good gifts unto your children, how much more shall your Father which is in heaven give good things to them that ask him?

Matthew 8:16-17

(16) When the even was come, they brought unto him many that were possessed with devils: and he cast out the spirits with his word, and healed all that were sick: (17) That it might be fulfilled which was spoken by Esaias the prophet, saying, Himself took our infirmities, and bare our sicknesses.

Matthew 9:35

(35) And Jesus went about all the cities and villages, teaching in their synagogues, and preaching the gospel of the kingdom, and healing every sickness and every disease among the people.

Matthew 15:30-31

(30) And great multitudes came unto him, having with them those that were lame, blind, dumb, maimed, and many others, and cast them down at Jesus' feet; and he healed them: (31)

Insomuch that the multitude wondered, when they saw the dumb to speak, the maimed to be whole, the lame to walk, and the blind to see: and they glorified the God of Israel.

Mark 11:22-24

(22) And Jesus answering saith unto them, Have faith in God. (23) For verily I say unto you, That whosoever shall say unto this mountain, Be thou removed, and be thou cast into the sea; and shall not doubt in his heart, but shall believe that those things which he saith shall come to pass; he shall have whatsoever he saith. (24) Therefore I say unto you, What things soever ye desire, when ye pray, believe that ye receive them, and ye shall have them.

Mark 16:17-18

(17) And these signs shall follow them that believe; In my name shall they cast out devils; they shall speak with new tongues; (18) They shall take up serpents; and if they drink any deadly thing, it shall not hurt them; they shall lay hands on the sick, and they shall recover.

Luke 4:17-19

(17) And there was delivered unto him the book of the prophet Esaias. And when he had opened the book, he found the place where it was written, (18) The Spirit of the Lord is upon me, because he hath anointed me to preach the gospel to the poor; he hath sent me to heal the brokenhearted, to preach deliverance to the captives, and recovering of sight to the blind, to set at liberty them that are bruised, (19) To preach the acceptable year of the Lord.

Luke 9:1-2

(1) Then he called his twelve disciples together, and gave them power and authority over all devils, and to cure diseases. (2)

And he sent them to preach the kingdom of God, and to heal the sick.

Luke 10:8-9

(8) And into whatsoever city ye enter, and they receive you, eat such things as are set before you: (9) And heal the sick that are therein, and say unto them, The kingdom of God is come nigh unto you.

Luke 13:16

(16) And ought not this woman, being a daughter of Abraham, whom Satan hath bound, lo, these eighteen years, be loosed from this bond on the Sabbath day?

Acts 4:29-30

(29) And now, Lord, behold their threatening: and grant unto thy servants, that with all boldness they may speak thy word, (30) By stretching forth thine hand to heal; and that signs and wonders may be done by the name of thy holy child Jesus.

Acts 5:15-16

(15) Insomuch that they brought forth the sick into the streets, and laid them on beds and couches, that at the least the shadow of Peter passing by might overshadow some of them. (16) There came also a multitude out of the cities round about unto Jerusalem, bringing sick folks, and them which were vexed with unclean spirits: and they were healed every one.

Acts 10:38

(38) How God anointed Jesus of Nazareth with the Holy Ghost and with power: who went about doing good, and healing all that were oppressed of the devil; for God was with him.

Galatians 3:13

(13) Christ hath redeemed us from the curse of the law, being made a curse for us: for it is written, Cursed is every one that hangeth on a tree:

James 5:13-16

(13) Is any among you afflicted? Let him pray. Is any merry? Let him sing psalms. (14) Is any sick among you? Let him call for the elders of the church; and let them pray over him, anointing him with oil in the name of the Lord: (15) And the prayer of faith shall save the sick, and the Lord shall raise him up; and if he have committed sins, they shall be forgiven him. (16) Confess your faults one to another, and pray one for another, that ye may be healed. The effectual fervent prayer of a righteous man availeth much.

1 John 5:14-15

(14) "And this is the confidence that we have in him, that, if we ask any thing according to his will, he heareth us: (15) And if we know that he hear us, whatsoever we ask, we know that we have the petitions that we desired of him.

3 John 2

"Beloved, I wish above all things that thou mayest prosper and be in health, even as thy soul prospereth.

RAYER REQUEST

Write down your prayer request below in the space provided. Record the time and date of each entry. When the Lord has answered your prayer request, be sure to describe how he answered you along with the date and time. All answers won't be what you want to hear, but what you need to hear, include those as well. Our Father knows best.

_____

_____

_____

_____

_____

_____

_____

_____

_____

_____

_____

_____

_____

_____

_____

References

Bourne, Edmund J.(2000). *The Anxiety & Phobia Workbook - Third Edition*. Oakland, CA: New Harbinger Publications, Inc.

Copeland, Kenneth (1989). *Covenant Made By Blood Study Guide*. Fort Worth, TX: Kenneth Copeland Publications

Goll, James W. (2007). *The Prophetic Intercessor Releasing God's Purposes to Change Lives and Influence Nations*. Grand Rapids, MI: Chosen Books.

Hammond, Frank & Ida Mae (2004). *Pigs In The Parlor*. Kirkwood, MO: Impact Christian Books, Inc.

Hamon, Bill (2008). *Prophets And Personal Prophecy God's Prophetic Voice Today*. Shippensburg, PA: Destiny Image Publishers, Inc.

Hormann, Aiko (1985). *Soul Restoration Healing of Inner Wounds*. Santa Monica, CA: Aiko Hormann Ministries.

MacNutt, Francis (2005). *Deliverance From Evil Spirits A Practical Manual*. Grand Rapids, MI: Chosen Books.

Mastin, Luke (2010). *The Human Memory. Memory Encoding*. http:// www.human-memory.net (accessed October, 2012).

Names of God (2003, 2005). Torrance, CA: Rose Publishing.

Price, Paula A. (2006). *The Prophet's Dictionary The Ultimate Guide to Supernatural Wisdom*. New Kensington, PA: Whitaker House.

Prince, Joseph (2007). *Destined To Reign*. Tulsa, OK: Harrison House.

Sumrall, Lester (1982). *The Gifts and Ministries Of The Holy Spirit*. New Kensington, PA: Whitaker House.

Sumrall, Lester (2003). *Demons: The Answer Book*. Kensington, PA: Whitaker House.

Smith, Melinda; Kemp, Gina; & Segal, Jeanne; (2012). *Laughter Is The Best Medicine. The Health Benefits of Humor*. http://www.helpguide.org/life/humor_laughter_health.htm (accessed October, 2012).

The American Heritage Dictionary, Second College Edition (1985). Boston: Houghton Mifflin Company.

The King James Study Bible (1988). Liberty University.

The Holy Bible, King James Version. Thomas Nelson, Inc.

The Holy Bible, New King James Version (1982). Thomas Nelson, Inc.

The Merriam-Webster Dictionary (1998). Merriam-Webster, Inc.

Van der Kolk, B., McFarlane, A., Weisaeth, L. (1996). *Traumatic Stress: The Effects of Overwhelming Experience On Mind, Body, And Society*. New York, NY: The Guilford Press.

Index

Jehovah-Sabaoth 7
Jehovah-Shalom 7
Jehovah-Shammah 7
Jehovah-Tsidkenu 8
Jehovan-Nissi 7
Jesus 3, 13, 15, 31, 39, 45, 50,
    56, 60, 63, 70, 77, 85, 87,
    94, 122, 125, 131, 148
Judah 119

K

King ix, 156
Kingdom 17, 38, 57, 75, 80, 85,
    89, 91, 122, 129, 133, 142,
    148, 150
Knowledge vii, 19, 40, 56, 69,
    73, 86, 90, 102, 120

L

Lamb 117
Laugh 33
Levitation 58
Life vii, ix, xii, 3, 15, 23, 30,
    34, 37, 45, 49, 55, 63, 77,
    85, 88, 92, 98, 100, 104,
    110, 118, 121, 130, 141,
    146
Light 118
Lion 119
Lord 3, 16, 26, 30, 37, 41, 46,
    49, 57, 59, 65, 69, 72, 76,
    86, 92, 97, 101, 104, 110,
    113, 115, 117, 127, 130,
    141
Lucifer 55
Lust 96, 99, 100

M

Magic 131

Magnify 74
Maladaptive 113
Mandate 136
Memories xii, 23
Mental xi, 17, 55, 139
Mercy 26, 50, 110, 120, 141
Minister 47, 71, 125
Miracles 69, 71, 131

N

New Age 131

O

Offended 29
Offering 125
Oil 47, 49, 121, 142, 151
Omega 3, 119

P

Physical xi, 17, 34, 55, 59, 95,
    130
Power vii, 3, 15, 31, 38, 45, 51,
    56, 58, 62, 71, 91, 95, 109,
    120, 123, 131, 136, 141,
    149
Praise 85, 115, 121, 124, 142
Prayer 15, 26, 30, 37, 45, 48,
    61, 65, 70, 72, 74, 105,
    122, 124, 130, 141, 143,
    151
Prayers ix, 29, 37, 40, 61, 99,
    120, 124, 141
Prince of Peace 119
Problem 110
Promise 62, 85, 89, 123, 130
Promises 75, 91, 123
Prophecy 39, 69, 72, 87, 155
Prophet 70, 72, 148, 155
Prophetic 40, 73, 155

Printed in the United States
By Bookmasters